MORMON PANTRY

Family Dinner Cookbook

More than 400 Simple & Delicious Recipes for Every Day of the Week

DEBBIE G. HARMAN

Substitution Guide

1/4 cup **brown sugar**---1/4 cup sugar + 2 Tbsp. maple syrup

1/4 cup **powdered sugar**---1/4 cup sugar (blend to powder in blender)

1 Tbsp. **baking powder**---1 tsp. baking soda + 2 tsp. cornstarch

1 **egg**---3 Tbsp. mayonnaise

1 Tbsp. **butter**---1 Tbsp. margarine

1/4 cup **vegetable oil**---1/2 cube butter or margarine, melted

1/4 cup **buttermilk**---1/4 cup milk + 1 Tbsp. vinegar

1/4 cup **cream**---1/4 cup canned milk

1/4 cup **canned milk**---1/4 cup milk + 1 Tbsp. dry milk

1/4 cup **sour cream**---3 Tbsp. milk + 1 Tbsp. vinegar + 1 Tbsp. butter

1/2 cup **cream of chicken soup**---1/3 cup white sauce + 1/4 cup chicken stock

1/2 cup **cream of celery soup**---1/3 cup white sauce + 1/4 cup chicken stock
  + 1/4 cup chopped celery

1/2 cup **cream of mushroom** soup---1/3 cup white sauce + 3 Tbsp. chopped
  mushrooms + 3 Tbsp. beef stock

1/4 cup **walnuts**---1/2 cup rolled oats

1 Tbsp. **red wine vinegar**---1 Tbsp. apple cider vinegar

1 Tbsp. **white wine vinegar**---1 Tbsp. white vinegar

1 Tbsp. **Worcestershire sauce**---2 tsp. soy sauce + 1 tsp. vinegar

Table of Contents

Time to Stock the Pantry

Stock your pantry with items that you will use often. Here is a list of some basic foods that you may want to keep in supply. These items frequently go on sale.

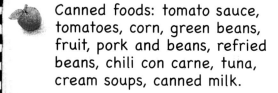 Canned foods: tomato sauce, tomatoes, corn, green beans, fruit, pork and beans, refried beans, chili con carne, tuna, cream soups, canned milk.

Dry goods: wheat, rice, oats, cornmeal, pastas, crackers, pinto beans, red beans.

Baking items: flour, salt, sugar, brown sugar, powdered sugar, baking powder, baking soda, yeast, dry milk, cornstarch.

Extra baking items: raisins, nuts, chocolate chips, cocoa, vanilla and other extracts.

Condiments: ketchup, mustard, mayonnaise, vinegar, soy sauce, Worcestershire sauce, pickles, olives, peanut butter, honey.

Planning Your Meals

- Plan a weekly menu using the advertised sales from your local grocers and using seasonal produce like squash, tomatoes, apples, etc.

- Use variety when planning meals. If you have a tomato-based meal like spaghetti one night, the next night plan a potato or white sauce base.

- Plan meals that will allow you to stay within your budget. Plan soups and casseroles for a few meals, but at least one nice meal each week.

- Plan a well-balanced menu. Make sure you cover the basic food groups. Plan your dinners first and then fill in missing nutrients with breakfast and lunch. Remember the reason we eat is to give our bodies the . . . NUTRIENTS THEY NEED! You will be healthier and happier if you prepare nutritious meals.

Don't Forget Your VITAMINS

VITAMIN-A ♥ For healthy skin and eyes boosts your immune system
SOURCES: sweet potatoes, carrots, squash, apricots, peaches red peppers, cantaloupe, spinach, broccoli, dairy products, eggs

VITAMIN-B
♥ Regulates appetite and digestion Healthy nervous system
Sources: Whole Wheat, Meat, Dairy

VITAMIN-C ♥ Strong bones and teeth, repairs cells. Helps to cure the common cold.
Sources: Bell Peppers, brussels sprouts, strawberries, oranges, broccoli, parsley, red cabbage, kiwifruit, and cauliflower.

VITAMIN-E ♥ Helps prevent Heart Disease and blood clots Builds red blood cells
Sources: Leafy greens, asparagus, wheat germ, peanuts almonds, butter, meat, sunflower seeds

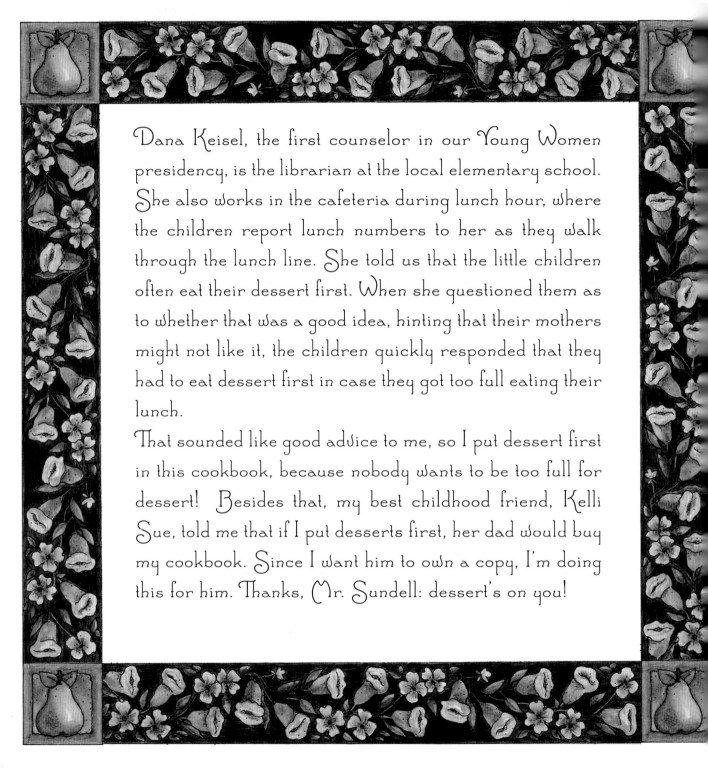

Dana Keisel, the first counselor in our Young Women presidency, is the librarian at the local elementary school. She also works in the cafeteria during lunch hour, where the children report lunch numbers to her as they walk through the lunch line. She told us that the little children often eat their dessert first. When she questioned them as to whether that was a good idea, hinting that their mothers might not like it, the children quickly responded that they had to eat dessert first in case they got too full eating their lunch.

That sounded like good advice to me, so I put dessert first in this cookbook, because nobody wants to be too full for dessert! Besides that, my best childhood friend, Kelli Sue, told me that if I put desserts first, her dad would buy my cookbook. Since I want him to own a copy, I'm doing this for him. Thanks, Mr. Sundell: dessert's on you!

Let's Do Desserts

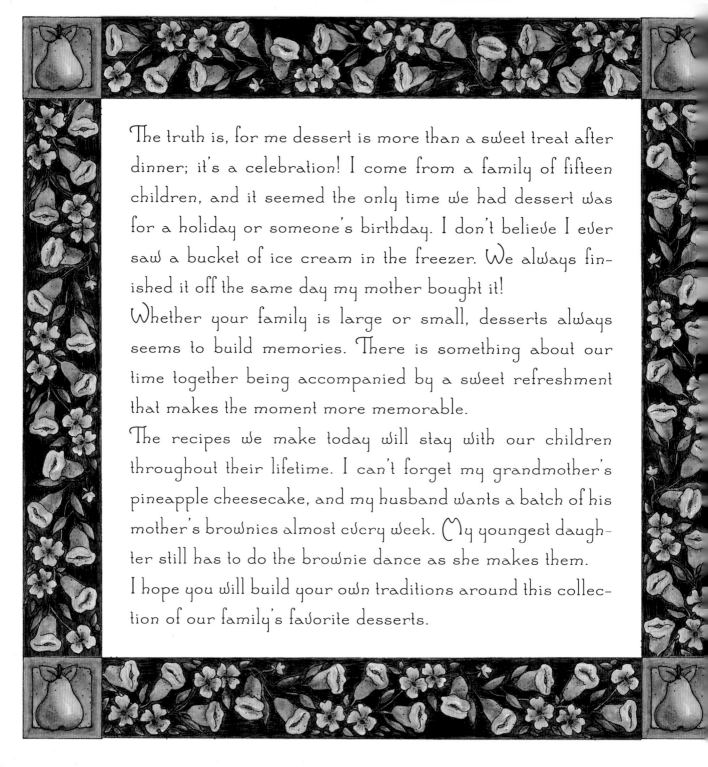

The truth is, for me dessert is more than a sweet treat after dinner; it's a celebration! I come from a family of fifteen children, and it seemed the only time we had dessert was for a holiday or someone's birthday. I don't believe I ever saw a bucket of ice cream in the freezer. We always finished it off the same day my mother bought it!

Whether your family is large or small, desserts always seems to build memories. There is something about our time together being accompanied by a sweet refreshment that makes the moment more memorable.

The recipes we make today will stay with our children throughout their lifetime. I can't forget my grandmother's pineapple cheesecake, and my husband wants a batch of his mother's brownies almost every week. My youngest daughter still has to do the brownie dance as she makes them.

I hope you will build your own traditions around this collection of our family's favorite desserts.

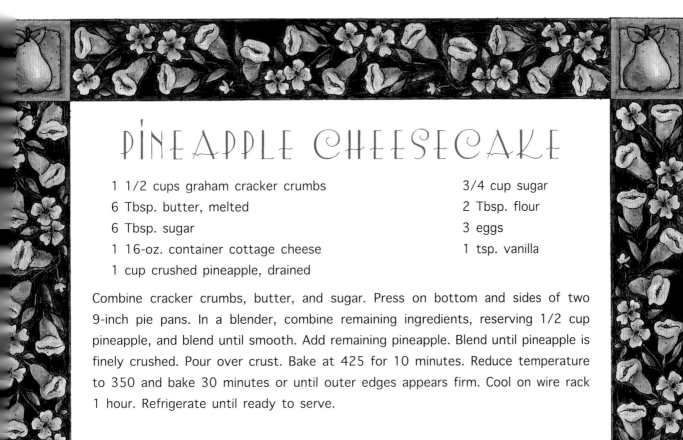

PINEAPPLE CHEESECAKE

1 1/2 cups graham cracker crumbs

6 Tbsp. butter, melted

6 Tbsp. sugar

1 16-oz. container cottage cheese

1 cup crushed pineapple, drained

3/4 cup sugar

2 Tbsp. flour

3 eggs

1 tsp. vanilla

Combine cracker crumbs, butter, and sugar. Press on bottom and sides of two 9-inch pie pans. In a blender, combine remaining ingredients, reserving 1/2 cup pineapple, and blend until smooth. Add remaining pineapple. Blend until pineapple is finely crushed. Pour over crust. Bake at 425 for 10 minutes. Reduce temperature to 350 and bake 30 minutes or until outer edges appears firm. Cool on wire rack 1 hour. Refrigerate until ready to serve.

CHEESECAKE SUPREME

Follow recipe for Pineapple Cheesecake, but replace cottage cheese with 3 8-oz. packages cream cheese and 1/4 cup milk. Replace pineapple with 1 Tbsp. lemon juice. Use hand mixer instead of blender to beat cream cheese. Mix remainder of ingredients with cream cheese until smooth. Bake and cool as directed. Top with blueberry, strawberry, cherry, or your favorite pie topping.

For Chocolate Swirl Cheesecake, stir 1/2 cup chocolate chips into batter after it has been poured into pie pan. Bake and cool as directed.

VANILLA CREAM PIE

1 9-inch pie shell, baked
1 cup sugar
1/3 cup flour
1/4 tsp. salt

3 cups milk
4 egg yolks
3 Tbsp. butter
2 tsp. vanilla

Bake pie shell at 450 for 10-12 minutes. Combine sugar, flour, and salt together in saucepan. Gradually stir in milk. Cook and stir over medium heat until thickened and bubbly. Remove from heat. Beat egg yolks slightly and mix with 1 cup cooked mixture. Pour back into pan and bring to a slow boil. Cook and stir 2 minutes more. Remove from heat. Stir in vanilla and pour into baked pie shell. Place plastic wrap over pudding to prevent skin from forming. Cool completely. Refrigerate until ready to serve. Top with whipped cream.

BANANA CREAM PIE

Follow directions for Vanilla Cream Pie, but slice 3 medium bananas into bottom of baked pie shell. Pour hot vanilla pudding over sliced bananas. Continue as directed.

12

CHOCOLATE CREAM PIE

Follow directions for Vanilla Cream Pie, except increase sugar to 1 1/4 cups and combine 1/2 cup cocoa powder with the sugar, flour, and salt. Continue as directed.

COCONUT CREAM PIE

Follow directions for Vanilla Cream Pie, but add 1 cup flaked coconut along with the vanilla. Continue as directed.

PERFECT PIE CRUST

1 1/3 cups all-purpose flour   1/2 cup cold butter
1/2 tsp. salt   3 Tbsp. cold water

Sift flour and salt together. Cut in cold butter until course and crumbly. Sprinkle in water 1 tablespoon at a time. Blend together with fork until dough forms into a ball. Roll out on lightly floured surface. Gently roll dough around rolling pin and lift over pie pan. Unroll dough and gently press down into sides and bottom of pan. Trim 1/2 inch wider than pan. Fold edge under and pinch to flute. Prick bottom and sides with fork. Bake according to pie directions. Makes one 9-inch pie crust.

13

CHOCOLATE SILK PIE

1 9-inch pie shell, unbaked
1 cup semi-sweet chocolate chips
1/2 cup butter
1/2 tsp. salt
1 cup sugar

1 Tbsp. cocoa powder
3 eggs
2/3 cup evaporated milk
1 tsp. vanilla

Melt butter and chocolate chips together in saucepan over medium heat. Mix in salt, sugar, and cocoa powder. Whisk eggs together with milk and vanilla until well blended. Add to chocolate mixture and stir well. Pour into pie shell. Bake at 350 for 30 minutes. Cool completely and refrigerate until ready to serve. Top with whipped topping and chocolate shavings if desired.

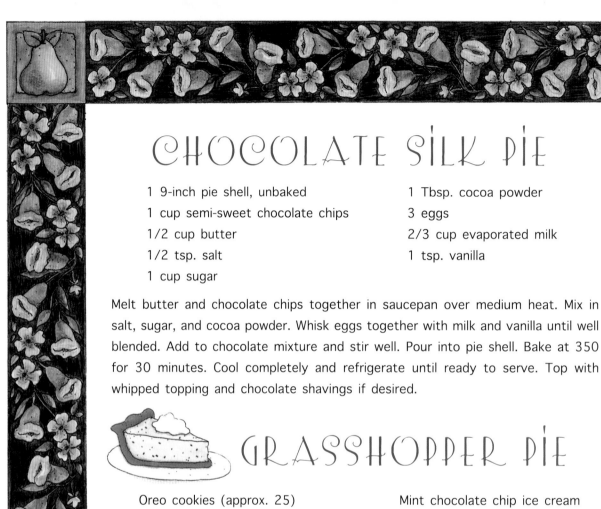

GRASSHOPPER PIE

Oreo cookies (approx. 25)
5 Tbsp. butter, melted
Chocolate shavings (opt.)

Mint chocolate chip ice cream
Whipped topping

Scrape frosting from cookies, then mash chocolate cookies to make 1 1/2 cups cookie crumbs. Mix with melted butter. Press into a 9-inch pie pan. Refrigerate 1 hour. Spread softened ice cream in pie shell. Spread whipped topping over ice cream. Sprinkle with chocolate shavings if desired. Freeze until ready to serve.

14

TIN ROOF SUNDAE PIE

1 chocolate cookie crust
1 cup mini chocolate chips
1 cup peanuts, coarsely ground
1/2 cup peanut butter

4 cups vanilla ice cream, softened
Whipped topping
Chocolate syrup

Follow recipe for crust from Grasshopper Pie recipe. Fold chocolate chips, peanuts, chocolate syrup, and peanut butter into ice cream. Spread in pie crust. Top with whipped topping if desired. Freeze until ready to serve.

KEY LIME PIE

1 9-inch pie shell, unbaked
3 egg yolks, whites discarded
1 14-oz. can sweetened condensed milk

3 tablespoons water
1/2 cup key lime juice
Whipped topping

Line unbaked pie shell with foil. Bake at 450 for 8 minutes. Allow pie shell to cool completely. Meanwhile, beat egg yolks with wire whisk or fork. Gradually stir in sweetened condensed milk and stir until well blended. Add lime juice, water, and a few drops green food coloring (optional). Mix well until mixture thickens. Pour into baked pie shell. Bake at 350 for 25 minutes. Cool on wire rack 1 hour. Refrigerate until ready to serve. Top with whipped topping if desired.

STRAWBERRY PIE

1 9-inch pie shell, unbaked
1/2 cup sugar
1 4-oz. pkg. strawberry Jell-O
3 Tbsp. cornstarch

1 1/4 cup water
1/4 cup lemon juice
4 cups strawberries, halved
Whipped topping

Bake pie shell at 450 for 10-12 minutes. Combine sugar, Jell-O, cornstarch, water, and lemon juice in a saucepan. Cook and stir over medium until mixture comes to a boil. Continue to stir while mixture boils, about 2 minutes or until mixture becomes transparent. Spread strawberries in cooled, baked pie shell. Pour Jell-O mixture over strawberries. Cover with plastic wrap and chill in refrigerator until ready to serve. Top with whipped topping if desired.

A mother is a person who, seeing there are only four pieces of pie for five people, promptly announces she never did care for pie.

Tenneva Jordan

WHIPPED TOPPING

Combine 1 cup whipping cream, 1 teaspoon vanilla, and 1/3 cup powdered sugar in small mixing bowl. Beat with an electric mixer until soft peaks form. Cover and refrigerate until ready to use.

FRESH PEACH PIE

1 1/4 cups water
4 cups peaches, peeled and sliced
1/2 cup sugar
1 4-oz. pkg. peach Jell-O

3 Tbsp. cornstarch
1/4 cup lemon juice
1 9-inch pie shell
Whipped topping

Bake pie shell at 450 for 10-12 minutes. Bring water to boil in large saucepan. Add peaches to boiling water and gently boil 2-3 minutes. Meanwhile, combine sugar, Jell-O, cornstarch, lemon juice, and 1 cup peach water in a separate bowl. Slowly add to peaches. Cook and stir over medium until mixture comes to a boil. Continue to stir while mixture boils, about 2 minutes or until mixture becomes transparent. Pour peach mixture into baked pie shell. Cool 5 minutes. Cover with plastic wrap and chill in refrigerator until ready to serve. Top with whipped topping if desired.

FRESH FRUIT TARTS

Follow recipe for Strawberry or Fresh Peach Pie, replacing baked pie shell with baked tart shells. Refrigerate until ready to serve. Top with whipped topping if desired.
Tart Shells: You can purchase small tart pans or use a muffin tin to make your tarts. Use the Perfect Pie Crust recipe. Cut dough to fit pans or muffin cups. Press dough into tart pans or muffin cups. Bake at 450 for 8-10 minutes or until golden brown. Cool on wire rack. Remove shells from pans and place on serving tray before filling.

STRAWBERRY CREAM PUFFS

1 cup water
1/2 cup butter
1/8 tsp. salt
1 cup flour
4 large eggs

Whipped topping
2 cups strawberries,
  hulled and sliced
1/4 cup sugar

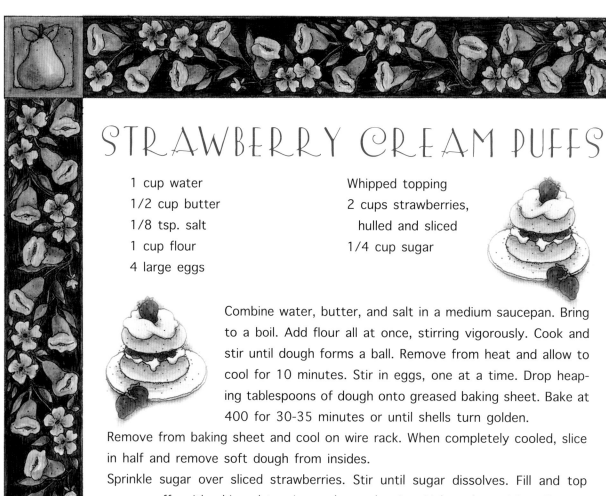

Combine water, butter, and salt in a medium saucepan. Bring to a boil. Add flour all at once, stirring vigorously. Cook and stir until dough forms a ball. Remove from heat and allow to cool for 10 minutes. Stir in eggs, one at a time. Drop heaping tablespoons of dough onto greased baking sheet. Bake at 400 for 30-35 minutes or until shells turn golden.

Remove from baking sheet and cool on wire rack. When completely cooled, slice in half and remove soft dough from insides.

Sprinkle sugar over sliced strawberries. Stir until sugar dissolves. Fill and top cream puffs with whipped topping and strawberries. Makes about 12 puffs.

BANANA CREAM PUFFS

Follow directions for Strawberry Cream Puffs, except slice 4 bananas. Place a few banana slices in each cream puff. Fill with vanilla pudding. Top with whipped topping.

APPLE CRUMB PIE

1 9-inch pie shell, unbaked
6 cups cooking apples,
  peeled and thinly sliced
1 Tbsp. lemon juice

3/4 cup sugar
2 Tbsp. flour
1/2 tsp. cinnamon
1/8 tsp. nutmeg

Sprinkle apples with lemon juice. Blend sugar, flour, cinnamon, and nutmeg together. Add apples and gently toss until coated. Spread apples in pie shell. Sprinkle with crumb mixture. Bake at 375 45-50 minutes or until crust is golden brown. Cool on wire rack.

Crumb Topping:
Stir together 1/2 cup flour and 1/2 cup brown sugar. Cut in 1/4 cup butter until coarse and crumbly.

PEACH CRUMB PIE

Follow above recipe, substituting peeled and sliced peaches for the apples. Increase nutmeg to 1/4 teaspoon and decrease cinnamon to 1/4 teaspoon. Continue as directed.

FRESH GINGER PUMPKIN PIE

1 1/2 cups sugar

1 tsp. salt

1 tsp. fresh grated ginger root

2 tsp. ground cinnamon

1/2 tsp. ground cloves

4 large eggs

1 29-oz. can pumpkin

1 cup whipping cream

1 1/2 cups milk

2 9-inch pie shells

Combine sugar, salt, and spices together. Whisk eggs in a large mixing bowl. Add pumpkin and sugar mixture and blend well. Gradually stir in cream and milk. Pour into unbaked pie shells. Bake at 425 for 15 minutes. Reduce temperature to 350 and bake additional 45 minutes. Cool on wire rack. Refrigerate until ready to serve.

Note: The secret ingredient to this delicious pie is the fresh ginger. Ginger root is sold in the produce section. It looks like a root. The cost will appear expensive, but because the root is so light in weight, it really only costs about 50 cents for a small root. Cut off the outer layer. Use the smallest grate on the grater to grate ginger (it is worth the effort!).

SWEET PECAN PUMPKIN PIE

Follow above recipe, but reduce cream and milk to 1/2 cup each. Prepare as directed, but bake at 375 for 25 minutes. Meanwhile, stir together 1 cup brown sugar, 1 cup chopped pecans, and 1/4 cup butter. Sprinkle mixture over pies and bake additional 20 minutes or until knife inserted at center comes out clean. Cool on wire rack. Refrigerate until ready to serve.

MOM'S CARROT CAKE

2 cups flour
2 cups sugar
1 tsp. baking powder
1 tsp. baking soda
1 tsp. cinnamon
1/4 tsp. salt

4 eggs, well beaten
3 cups carrots, finely shredded
3/4 cup vegetable oil
1/2 cup walnuts, chopped (opt.)
1 cup raisins (opt.)
Cream Cheese frosting

Sift together flour, sugar, baking powder, baking soda, cinnamon, and salt. In a separate bowl whisk together eggs, carrots, and oil. Add to flour mixture and stir until well blended. Stir in nuts and raisins if desired. Pour into greased 9x13 cake pan and bake at 350 for 35-40 minutes or until knife inserted at center comes out clean. Cool on wire rack. Frost with Cream Cheese Frosting

CREAM CHEESE FROSTING

1 4-oz. pkg. cream cheese
4 Tbsp. butter, softened

1 tsp. vanilla
3 cups powdered sugar

Beat cream cheese with an electric mixer until smooth. Add softened butter and vanilla and mix until well blended. Gradually mix in powdered sugar until frosting reaches a nice spreading consistency. Makes about 2 cups frosting.

LAYERED CREAM CAKE

1 yellow cake mix
1/2 cup flour
1/4 cup sugar
3 eggs
1/3 cup oil
1 1/3 cups water

2 cups vanilla pudding
1 cup whipping cream
1/2 cup powdered sugar
1 tsp. vanilla
2 cups fresh or frozen fruit
1/2 cup sugar

Oil and flour two 9-inch cake pans. Line bottoms with waxed paper. Sift cake mix, flour, and 1/4 cup sugar in mixing bowl. Add eggs, oil, and water; beat with electric mixer 3-4 minutes. Pour into prepared cake pans. Using a spatula, pull batter up at sides, leaving a valley in the center. This will make the cake even across the top rather than raised in the center. Bake at 350 for 20-25 minutes.

Cool on wire rack. Cut top to be level with pan sides. Remove cake from pans and remove waxed paper. Using a serrated knife, slice cakes in half horizontally. Place first level on cake platter. Spread 1/3 vanilla pudding over cake. Place another cake layer on pudding and repeat until the top layer of cake. Whip the cream, powdered sugar and vanilla together until soft peaks form. Spread whipped cream over top layer of cake. Sprinkle fruit (strawberries, raspberries, blueberries, etc.) with sugar. Spoon fruit over cake just before serving.

BOSTON CREAM CAKE

Follow recipe for Layered Cream Cake but do not spread whipped cream on top layer. Instead, pour chocolate glaze over top, allowing it to drizzle down the sides.

Chocolate Glaze:
In a small saucepan, combine 1/2 cup light cream or whipping cream, 1/3 cup semi-sweet chocolate chips, and 2 Tbsp. sugar. Cook and stir over low heat until chocolate chips melt and mixture is melted and slightly thickened. Cool slightly before drizzling over cake.

COCONUT CREAM CAKE

Follow recipe for Layered Cream Cake; sprinkle flaked coconut over each layer of vanilla pudding. Spread whipped cream on top of cake. Sprinkle toasted coconut lightly over whipped cream.

Toasted coconut:
Spread 1/2 cup coconut on shallow baking pan. Broil until coconut starts to turn golden brown (watch closely).

LEMON POPPY SEED CAKE

1 cup butter, softened

2 1/2 cups flour

2 tsp. baking powder

1/2 tsp. salt

1 3/4 cups sugar

4 large eggs, room temperature

1 tsp. vanilla extract

1 tsp. lemon extract

3/4 cup milk, room temperature

1/4 cup poppy seeds

Butter and flour two 8" round cake pans. Line bottom of cake pans with waxed paper. Sift together flour, baking powder, and salt. Cream butter with electric mixer. Gradually add sugar. Mix in eggs after each addition. Beat in vanilla and lemon extract. Add flour mixture and milk alternately, and beat on low speed after each addition. Stir in poppy seeds. Pour batter into pans and bake at 350 for 35-45 minutes or until knife inserted in middle comes out clean. Cool on wire rack. Remove cakes from pans and peel off waxed paper. Place one cake layer on cake platter and spread Cream Cheese Frosting over top. Place second layer on top and frost. When ready to serve, pour Lemon Poppy Seed Glaze over top, allowing it to drizzle down sides.

Cream Cheese Frosting:

Beat 1 8-oz. package cream cheese with electric mixer until smooth. Add 1/4 cup butter and 2 cups powdered sugar; mix on low speed until smooth.

Lemon Poppy Seed Glaze:

Stir together 1 cup powdered sugar, 3 Tbsp. lemon juice, and 1 1/2 tsp. poppy seeds. Add more lemon juice if needed.

24

YUMMY POPPY SEED CAKE

Follow recipe for Lemon Poppy Seed Cake, substituting rum extract for the lemon extract. Do not frost between layers, but use glaze between layers.
For glaze, melt 1/4 cup butter in medium saucepan. Stir in 1/4 cup cream or milk and 1 teaspoon butter or rum flavoring. Add 2 cups powdered sugar and stir until smooth. Stir in poppy seeds and pour over cake while glaze is still warm. If needed, add more cream or milk to glaze.

POPPY SEED ALMOND CAKE

Follow recipe for Lemon Poppy Seed Cake, substituting almond extract for the lemon extract. Replace glaze with recipe below.
Glaze:
Mix 1 cup powdered sugar, 1/4 cup orange juice, 1/2 teaspoon vanilla, and 1/2 teaspoon almond extract together. Beat until smooth. Drizzle over cake layers. Sprinkle with sliced almonds, if desired.

25

CHOCOLATE ECLAIRS

1 cup water
1/2 cup butter
1/8 tsp. salt
1 cup flour
4 large eggs

Chocolate pudding
Whipped topping
1 cup chocolate chips
3 Tbsp. butter
1/2 tsp. vanilla

Combine water, butter, and salt in a medium saucepan. Bring to a boil. Add flour all at once, stirring rapidly. Cook and stir until dough forms a ball. Remove from heat and allow to cool for 10 minutes. Stir in eggs, one at a time, beating until thoroughly blended. Cut a hole 1/2-inch wide at corner of quart-size freezer bag. Place dough in bag and squeeze dough through hole onto greased baking sheet. Eclairs should be 4 inches long, 1 inch wide, and 3/4 inches high. Bake at 400 for 30-35 minutes or until golden brown. Remove from baking sheet and cool on wire rack. When completely cooled, slice in half and remove soft dough from insides. Fill bottoms with chocolate pudding (follow recipe from Chocolate Cream Pie) and replace tops. Drizzle chocolate glaze over tops.

Chocolate Glaze:

Melt chocolate chips and butter over low heat, continually stirring until chocolate is completely melted. Remove from heat and stir in vanilla. Cool slightly but drizzle over eclairs while glaze is still warm.

Note: You can use vanilla, butterscotch, or other puddings in this recipe.

LITTLE LAVA CAKES

1 3/4 cups semi-sweet chocolate chips
2 Tbsp. whipping cream
3 eggs
3 egg yolks
1/3 cup sugar

1 1/2 tsp. vanilla
1/3 cup flour
3 Tbsp. cocoa powder
Powdered sugar

Melt 3/4 cup chocolate chips and whipping cream in a saucepan. Cook and stir over low heat until chocolate chips are completely melted. Remove from heat. Cool in saucepan, stirring occasionally. Cover and place in refrigerator until firm. Shape chocolate into 6 balls of equal size. In separate saucepan, melt remaining chocolate chips with butter over low heat. Remove from heat and cool. Whisk together eggs, egg yolks, sugar, and vanilla until mixture turns light yellow. Add chocolate and beat until smooth. Add flour and cocoa and mix until well blended. Spoon 2 Tablespoons batter into greased muffin cups. Place 1 chocolate ball in each muffin cup. Spoon remaining batter into cups. Bake at 400 for 10-12 minutes or until batter is firm around edges. Cool on wire rack 2-3 minutes. Loosen cakes from sides. Carefully remove cakes and invert onto dessert plates. Sprinkle with powdered sugar. Serve while still warm.

Laughter is brightest where food is best...

Food is best where love is served.

27

TEXAS SHEET CAKE

2 cups all-purpose flour

2 cups sugar

1 tsp. baking soda

1/4 tsp. salt

1 cup butter

1/3 cup cocoa powder

2 eggs

1/2 cup buttermilk

1 1/2 tsp. vanilla

Chocolate Buttermilk Icing

Sift first four ingredients together. Melt butter in medium saucepan. Stir in cocoa and water. Pour into flour mixture and beat until smooth. Add eggs, buttermilk, and vanilla and mix until well blended. Pour into greased 10x15 sheet cake pan. Bake at 350 for 25-30 minutes. Remove from oven and frost while still warm.

Chocolate Buttermilk Icing:

Melt 1/4 cup butter in a small saucepan. Add 3 Tbsp. cocoa powder and 3 Tbsp. buttermilk. Bring to a boil. Remove from heat and stir in 2 1/4 cups powdered sugar and 1/2 teaspoon vanilla. Beat until smooth. Add 3/4 cup chopped walnuts if desired. Spread quickly over warm sheet cake.

ICE CREAM CAKE ROLL

Follow above recipe or use 2 boxed cake mixes. Before baking, cover bottom of pan with waxed paper. Bake as directed. Cool on wire rack. Spread softened ice cream (any flavor) over cake. Cut cake in half widthwise. Roll each side jelly-roll style, peeling off wax paper as you roll. Wrap tightly with foil and freeze.

ICE CREAM SANDWICH LAYERED CAKE

12 ice cream sandwiches
2-quart carton tin roof sundae
   ice cream, softened

Whipped topping
Chocolate ice cream syrup
Butterfingers, broken up

Remove wrappers from ice cream sandwiches. Place 6 sandwiches on bottom of 9x13 pan. Completely open carton of ice cream. Cut ice cream into 1/2-inch slices and place them over sandwiches until they are completely covered. Spread ice cream until fairly even. Place a second layer of sandwiches over the layer of ice cream. Spread whipped topping over sandwiches. Freeze until ready to serve. Before serving, drizzle with chocolate topping and sprinkle with Butterfinger pieces.

Other tasty combinations:

Butter brickle or praline ice cream with caramel topping and Score candy bar pieces.

Mint chocolate chip ice cream with chocolate syrup and broken Andes mints.

Neapolitan ice cream sandwiches with Neapolitan ice cream. Top with whipped topping, sliced bananas, and chocolate, strawberry, and pineapple toppings; place a cherry on top of each serving.

29

Sunday has always been my favorite day of the week. I love to go to church where we visit with friends and neighbors and learn together. I appreciate the weekly reminder of what is most important. I enjoy coming home and having all of my family share what we learned. I even look forward to any Sunday service that might be required of us. I guess I really just cherish the overall reverence that I feel for the Sabbath. I want that special feeling to last throughout the day, so I try to make meals that seem special yet are simple to make.

The following pages are filled with some Sunday dinner recipes. As you make these dishes, keep in mind that many of them can be prepared ahead of time or cooked while you are away from home. They can be accompanied by any of the bread or roll recipes found in the soup and bread section.

I hope you this Sunday dinner menu collection helps make your day special.

Sunday

Dinner Menus

OVEN ROASTED TURKEY

4- to 5-pound turkey breast
1 tsp. poultry seasoning
1 Tbsp. parsley flakes

1/4 cup butter
1 cup water
1 pkg. stuffing mix

Rinse turkey breast and pat dry. Rub with poultry seasoning. Place in roasting pan or baking dish and sprinkle parsley on top. Cover with lid or foil. Bake at 250 for 3-4 hours or until meat is no longer pink when cut in center. Mix butter, water, and stuffing. Spread over top of turkey breast. Cook additional hour or until meat thermometer reads 170 at center. Let stand 10 minutes before slicing. Serve with stuffing and choice of vegetables.

TURKEY GRAVY

1 cup turkey drippings
3 cups water

1 tsp. chicken bouillon (opt.)
1/3 cup flour

In a medium saucepan, stir flour into turkey drippings until well blended. Add water and, if desired, chicken bouillon. Cook and stir over medium heat until thickened and bubbly. Remove from heat and pour into gravy boat. Gravy will continue to thicken as it cools, so always make it a little thinner than desired.

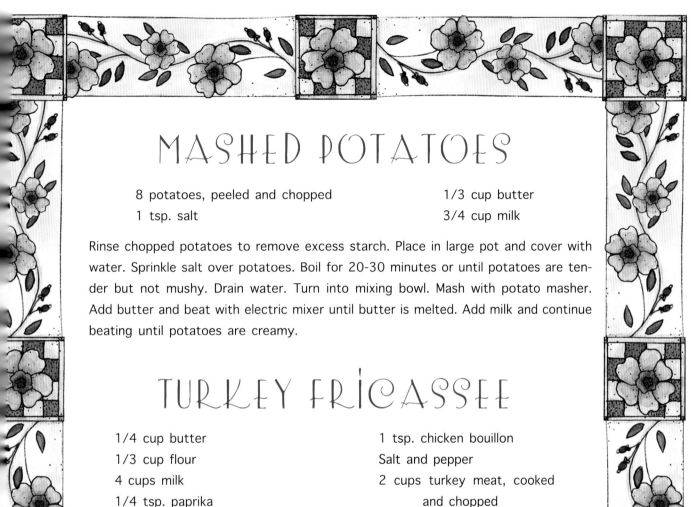

MASHED POTATOES

8 potatoes, peeled and chopped   1/3 cup butter
1 tsp. salt   3/4 cup milk

Rinse chopped potatoes to remove excess starch. Place in large pot and cover with water. Sprinkle salt over potatoes. Boil for 20-30 minutes or until potatoes are tender but not mushy. Drain water. Turn into mixing bowl. Mash with potato masher. Add butter and beat with electric mixer until butter is melted. Add milk and continue beating until potatoes are creamy.

TURKEY FRICASSEE

1/4 cup butter   1 tsp. chicken bouillon
1/3 cup flour   Salt and pepper
4 cups milk   2 cups turkey meat, cooked
1/4 tsp. paprika   and chopped

Melt butter in medium saucepan. Stir in flour until smooth. Slowly add milk, stirring constantly. Add paprika, salt, and pepper to desired taste. Cook and stir over medium heat until thickened and bubbly. Stir in turkey meat and heat through. Serve over mashed potatoes.

33

TOMATO~BASIL CHICKEN

8 boneless, skinless chicken breast halves

2 cups yogurt

1 10-oz. box Tomato-Basil Wheat Thins

1/2 cup Parmesan cheese, grated

1/2 tsp. garlic powder

1/2 tsp. salt

1/4 tsp. pepper

1 Tbsp. parsley flakes

Chicken Sauce:

1 can cream of chicken soup

1 cup milk

Rinse chicken breast halves and pat dry. Pour yogurt into small dish. Crush crackers into fine crumbs. In a separate dish, blend cracker crumbs with Parmesan cheese and seasonings. Dip chicken breast halves into yogurt, coating both sides. Roll in crumbs until well covered. Place in greased baking pan. Repeat with remaining breast halves. Bake at 350 for 1 hour or until chicken is done. For sauce, combine soup and milk in a saucepan and cook over medium heat until hot until bubbly. Serve over chicken.

TWICE~BAKED POTATOES

Cut 8 baked potatoes lengthwise. Scoop insides into bowl and save skins. Mash potatoes with 1/3 cup butter, salt, and pepper. Stir in 1/2 cup sour cream and 1 cup shredded cheddar cheese. Return potatoes to skins. Place on baking sheet. Bake at 425 for 15-20 minutes or until cheese is melted.

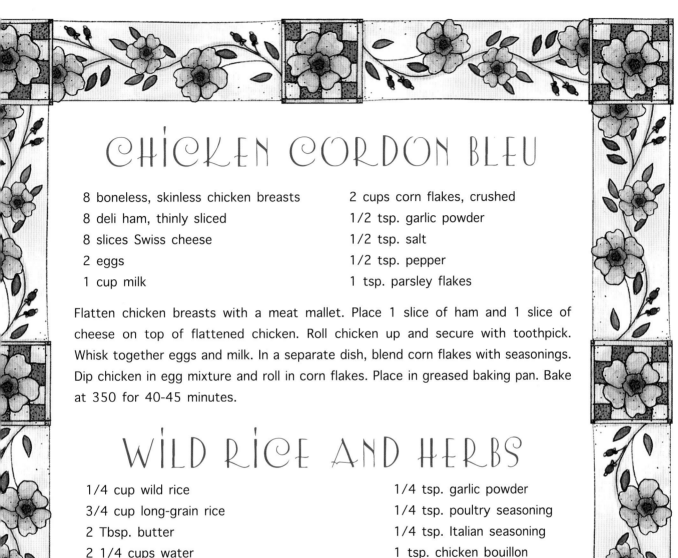

CHICKEN CORDON BLEU

8 boneless, skinless chicken breasts

8 deli ham, thinly sliced

8 slices Swiss cheese

2 eggs

1 cup milk

2 cups corn flakes, crushed

1/2 tsp. garlic powder

1/2 tsp. salt

1/2 tsp. pepper

1 tsp. parsley flakes

Flatten chicken breasts with a meat mallet. Place 1 slice of ham and 1 slice of cheese on top of flattened chicken. Roll chicken up and secure with toothpick. Whisk together eggs and milk. In a separate dish, blend corn flakes with seasonings. Dip chicken in egg mixture and roll in corn flakes. Place in greased baking pan. Bake at 350 for 40-45 minutes.

WILD RICE AND HERBS

1/4 cup wild rice

3/4 cup long-grain rice

2 Tbsp. butter

2 1/4 cups water

1/4 tsp. garlic powder

1/4 tsp. poultry seasoning

1/4 tsp. Italian seasoning

1 tsp. chicken bouillon

Place rice, water, and seasonings in a medium saucepan. Bring to a boil over medium-high heat. Reduce heat to low and cover with tight-fitting lid. Cook 20 minutes, stirring occasionally, or until rice is tender (add more water if necessary).

CURRIED CHICKEN

8 boneless, skinless chicken breast halves

1/4 cup butter

1 onion, finely diced

1/2 cup green pepper, diced

1 cup raisins

1 tsp. curry powder

1 can cream of chicken soup

1 cup milk

Place chicken breast in greased casserole dish. Saute onions and peppers until onions turn transparent. Combine with remaining ingredients and pour over chicken. Bake at 350 for 1 hour.

GARLIC POTATOES

8 potatoes, peeled and chopped

1 tsp. salt

1/3 cup butter

2/3 cup sour cream

3/4 cup milk

1/2 tsp. garlic powder

Rinse chopped potatoes to remove excess starch. Place in large pot and cover with water. Sprinkle salt over potatoes. Boil for 20-30 minutes or until potatoes are tender but not mushy. Drain water. Turn into mixing bowl. Mash with potato masher. Add butter and beat with electric mixer until butter is melted. Add sour cream, milk, and garlic powder, and continue mixing until potatoes are creamy.

APRICOT CHICKEN

6 medium chicken breasts
1 1/2 cups apricot jam
1/3 cup lemon juice

1 tsp. nutmeg
Salt and pepper

Place chicken breasts in casserole dish. Mix apricot jam, lemon juice, and nutmeg. Sprinkle chicken with salt and pepper. Spread apricot sauce over chicken. Cover with foil. Bake at 375 for 45 minutes. Remove foil and bake an additional 15 minutes. Serve with Herbed Rice and Roni (below).

HERBED RICE AND RONI

3/4 cup vermicelli pieces, broken
3/4 cup long-grain rice
2 Tbsp. butter
2 1/2 cups water

1/4 tsp. garlic powder
1/4 tsp. poultry seasoning
1/4 tsp. Italian seasoning
1 tsp. chicken bouillon

Saute vermicelli (thin spaghetti) and rice in butter until vermicelli starts to brown. Add water and seasonings and mix well. Bring to a boil over medium-high heat. Reduce heat to low and cover with tight-fitting lid. Cook 20 minutes, stirring occasionally, or until rice is tender (add more water if necessary).

SUNDAY DINNER ROAST

4- to 5-pound beef roast   Beef bouillon or Kitchen Bouquet

When selecting a roast, look for some marbling (thin veins of white fat through-out the meat) in the beef. This will make the meat more tender and flavorful. Place the roast in roasting or baking pan. Rub bouillon or Kitchen Bouquet on roast. (Note: You can also use au jus or beef gravy mix.) Make a tent out of foil and place over the roast. Cover with lid or more foil and bake at 350 for 3 hours. Baste with juices. Allow to cool 10-15 minutes before slicing. Serve with mashed potatoes and brown gravy, Easy Cooked Carrots and Steamed Peas.

EASY COOKED CARROTS

6 carrots, peeled and sliced   Salt and pepper
1 cup water   1 tsp. butter (opt.)

Place carrots and water in a saucepan. Sprinkle with salt and pepper. Cover with tight-fitting lid and cook, stirring occasionally, at medium-low heat for 20 minutes or until carrots are tender. Drain and serve with butter if desired.

38

OVEN ROAST WITH VEGGIES

4- to 5-pound beef roast

2 tsp. beef bouillon

1 pound baby carrots

6 potatoes, peeled and chopped

1 medium onion, chopped

Follow directions for Sunday Dinner Roast, but place prepared vegetables around roast in Dutch oven or roasting pan before cooking. Cook as directed. Baste roast and allow 10-15 minutes to cool before slicing. Place slices in center of serving tray. Remove vegetables carefully and place them around roast on serving tray or serve them in a separate dish. Serve with one of the roll recipes found in the soup and bread section.

BEST BROWN GRAVY

Meat drippings from roast

3 cups water

1 tsp. Kitchen Bouquet

1/3 cup flour

In a medium saucepan, stir flour into meat drippings until well blended. Add water and Kitchen Bouquet. Cook and stir over medium heat until thickened and bubbly. Remove from heat and pour into gravy boat. Gravy will continue to thicken as it cools, so always make it a little thinner than desired.

SALISBURY STEAKS

2 pounds ground beef

1 cup dry bread crumbs

1 cup milk

2 eggs

Salt and pepper

1/2 cup onion, finely diced

2 tsp. Worcestershire sauce

1/4 tsp. garlic powder

1/2 cup mushrooms, sliced

Combine meat with remaining ingredients except mushrooms. Shape into 10-12 patties. Cook patties in a skillet three at a time. Place cooked patties in a baking dish and keep warm in the oven. Continue cooking patties until all are done. Prepare Best Brown Gravy. Stir in sliced mushrooms. Pour gravy over steaks. Serve with Broccoli and Cheese Sauce.

BROCCOLI AND SAUCE

4 cups broccoli, chopped

1/4 cup butter

1/3 cup flour

3 cups milk

2 cups cheese, grated

1/2 tsp. salt

Steam broccoli until tender. In separate saucepan, melt butter. Stir in flour until smooth. Slowly add milk. Cook and stir over medium heat until thickened and bubbly. Add cheese and salt and continue cooking and stirring until cheese is melted and sauce is smooth. Serve over steamed broccoli.

40

SEASONED MEATLOAF

2 pounds ground beef
2 eggs, well beaten
20 saltine crackers, crushed
1 16-oz. can tomato sauce
1/2 cup onion, finely diced

1/4 cup green pepper, diced
1 tsp. salt
1 tsp. garlic powder
1 tsp. Italian seasoning
Ketchup

Combine meat with remaining ingredients except ketchup. Press into a 9x13 pan. Bake at 350 for 1 hour. Remove from oven and let cool 5 minutes. Soak up excess fat with a paper towel. Spread ketchup over top and return to oven. Bake at 425 for 10 minutes. Serve with scalloped potatoes.

SCALLOPED POTATOES

6-8 potatoes, unpeeled
1/2 cup finely diced onions
1/4 cup butter

1 cup sour cream
2 cups cheese, grated
2 Tbsp. vinegar

Boil unpeeled potatoes 20-30 minutes or until tender, but firm. Remove from heat. Allow to cool. Meanwhile, saute onions in butter until they start to turn brown. Mix onions with sour cream, cheese, and vinegar in casserole dish and stir well. Peel and thinly slice potatoes. Fold potatoes into sauce. Bake at 350 for 30 minutes.

SWEET PORK CHOPS

8 boneless pork chops
2 Tbsp. vegetable oil
1/2 cup brown sugar
1/2 cup sweet onion, chopped

1/2 cup barbecue sauce
1/2 cup ketchup
1/2 cup honey
1/2 cup French dressing

Brown pork chops in oil. Place in baking dish. Combine remaining ingredients and pour over pork chops. Bake at 350 for 40-45 minutes. Serve with Special Green Beans.

SPECIAL GREEN BEANS

2 16-oz. cans green beans
1/4 cup butter

1 4-oz. pkg. slivered almonds
Salt and pepper

Combine all ingredients in a medium saucepan. Cook over medium heat, stirring occasionally, until butter is melted and liquid starts to boil slightly.

STEAMED PEAS

Place 3 cups fresh or frozen peas and 3/4 cup water in a medium saucepan. Steam over medium-low heat just until peas are heated through. Don't overcook.

BAKED MUSHROOM CHOPS

8 pork chops
2 cans cream of mushroom soup
1 can mushrooms, pieces and stems

1 1/2 cups sour cream
1 cup milk
Salt and pepper

Brown pork chops in oil. Place in baking dish. Combine remaining ingredients and pour over pork chops. Bake at 350 for 40-45 minutes. Serve with Steamed Peas and Buttery Herbed Noodles (below).

Let every person in the family, who is able, make one part of the meal. This keeps preparation simple.

BUTTERY HERBED NOODLES

1 12-oz. pkg. wide egg noodles
1/4 cup butter
1/2 tsp. salt

1 tsp. parsley flakes
1/2 tsp. poultry seasoning
1/2 tsp. Italian seasoning

Cook egg noodles according to package directions. Drain noodles. Melt butter. Add seasonings to melted butter and saute for 1 minute. Return noodles to pan and stir until well coated with butter and seasonings.

43

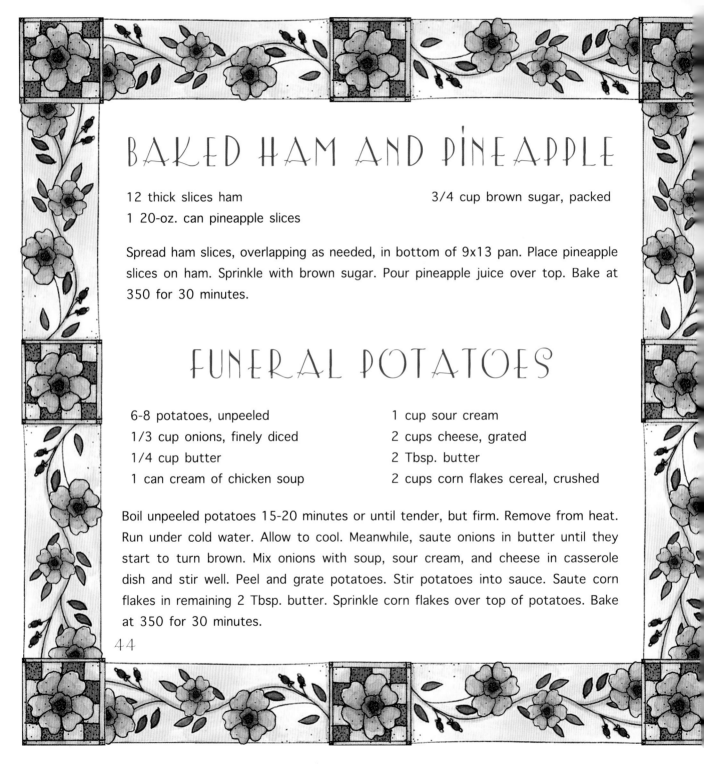

BAKED HAM AND PINEAPPLE

12 thick slices ham

3/4 cup brown sugar, packed

1 20-oz. can pineapple slices

Spread ham slices, overlapping as needed, in bottom of 9x13 pan. Place pineapple slices on ham. Sprinkle with brown sugar. Pour pineapple juice over top. Bake at 350 for 30 minutes.

FUNERAL POTATOES

6-8 potatoes, unpeeled

1/3 cup onions, finely diced

1/4 cup butter

1 can cream of chicken soup

1 cup sour cream

2 cups cheese, grated

2 Tbsp. butter

2 cups corn flakes cereal, crushed

Boil unpeeled potatoes 15-20 minutes or until tender, but firm. Remove from heat. Run under cold water. Allow to cool. Meanwhile, saute onions in butter until they start to turn brown. Mix onions with soup, sour cream, and cheese in casserole dish and stir well. Peel and grate potatoes. Stir potatoes into sauce. Saute corn flakes in remaining 2 Tbsp. butter. Sprinkle corn flakes over top of potatoes. Bake at 350 for 30 minutes.

44

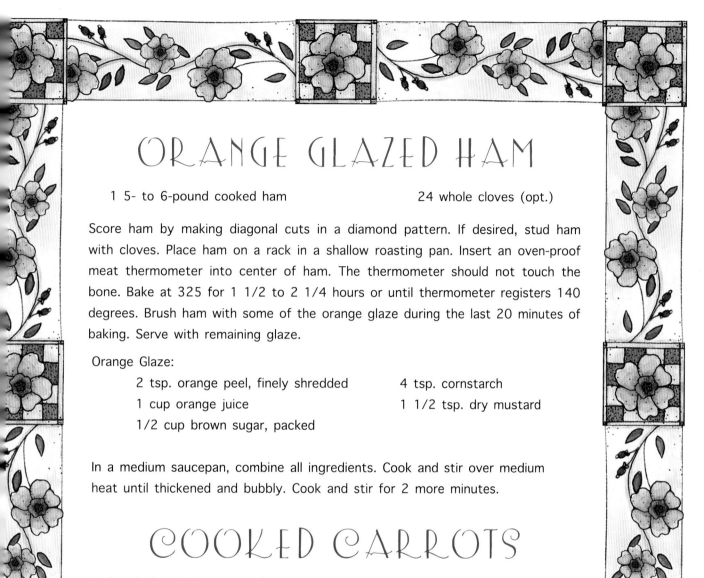

ORANGE GLAZED HAM

1 5- to 6-pound cooked ham   24 whole cloves (opt.)

Score ham by making diagonal cuts in a diamond pattern. If desired, stud ham with cloves. Place ham on a rack in a shallow roasting pan. Insert an oven-proof meat thermometer into center of ham. The thermometer should not touch the bone. Bake at 325 for 1 1/2 to 2 1/4 hours or until thermometer registers 140 degrees. Brush ham with some of the orange glaze during the last 20 minutes of baking. Serve with remaining glaze.

Orange Glaze:

2 tsp. orange peel, finely shredded   4 tsp. cornstarch
1 cup orange juice   1 1/2 tsp. dry mustard
1/2 cup brown sugar, packed

In a medium saucepan, combine all ingredients. Cook and stir over medium heat until thickened and bubbly. Cook and stir for 2 more minutes.

COOKED CARROTS

Peel and slice 6-8 carrots. Place in medium saucepan with 1 cup water. Sprinkle with salt. Cover and cook on medium-low heat 20 minutes or until tender. If desired, serve with butter melted on top.

45

The crockpot (now called the slow cooker) is one of my favorite ways to cook. Not only is it convenient to be able to put your ingredients together in the morning and end up with a finished meal at night, but it is also a great way to get a flavorful blend from foods that is not possible when the foods are cooked quickly. I have also tried many Dutch oven recipes from expert Dutch oven cookers, and have found that they work well in the crockpot.

The next few pages feature a collection of some of my family's favorite crockpot recipes. I always use the high setting when making these recipes, but if you are going to be away from home, you should use the low setting and allow the longer cooking time. You can use some of the bread recipes from the soup section to go along with these crockpot meals.

Monday

Crockpot Meals

DUTCH OVEN CHICKEN

4 medium boneless, skinless chicken breasts
1 tsp. chicken bouillon
1 pound baby carrots
6 medium potatoes, peeled and chopped
1 onion, chopped

2 stalks celery, sliced (opt.)
Salt and pepper
2 cans cream of mushroom soup
1 cup sour cream
1 cup milk

Place chicken in crock pot and sprinkle with bouillon. Add remaining ingredients in order given. Cook on high 4-5 hours or low 7-8 hours. Cut chicken into smaller chunks before serving.

HEARTY BAKED BEANS

6 slices bacon, cut into 1/2-inch pieces
1 pound hamburger, browned and drained
3 16-oz. cans pork and beans, drained
1 16-oz. can kidney beans, drained
1/2 onion, chopped

1/2 green bell pepper, chopped
1/2 cup ketchup
3 Tbsp. mustard
1/2 cup brown sugar
2 Tbsp. Worcestershire sauce

Cook bacon until almost done in crock pot. Do not drain. Add remaining ingredients and stir well. Cook on high 2-3 hours or low 4-5 hours.

48

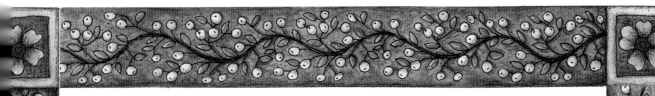

DUTCH OVEN POTATOES

4 slices bacon, chopped
8 potatoes, thinly sliced
1 onion, thinly sliced

2 cans cream of mushroom soup
1 cup sour cream
1 cup milk

Place all ingredients in crock pot. Sprinkle with salt and pepper. Cook on high 4-5 hours or low 7-8 hours.

A hundred men may make an encampment, but it takes a woman to make a home.

Chinese Proverb

SLOPPY JOES

2 pounds hamburger
1/2 envelope Sloppy Joe seasoning mix
1 carrot, peeled and shredded
2 stalks celery, finely chopped
1/2 onion, finely chopped

1/2 cup ketchup
1/4 cup mustard
1/4 cup sugar
3 8-oz. cans tomato sauce
1 dozen hamburger buns

Cook hamburger with salt, pepper, and garlic powder. Drain fat. Add remaining ingredients and stir well. Cook on high 2-3 hours or low 4-5 hours. Serve on hamburger buns.

49

VEGETABLE BEEF STEW

2- to 3-pound boneless beef roast

2 tsp. beef bouillon

1/4 cup all-purpose flour

1 1-pound pkg. baby carrots

6 medium potatoes, peeled and chopped

1 onion, chopped

2 stalks celery, sliced

1 tsp. Italian seasoning

1 cup water

1 cup frozen peas

Place roast in crock pot and rub bouillon over top. Sprinkle flour over roast. Add remaining ingredients except peas in order given. Cook on high 4-5 hours or low for 7-8 hours. Remove roast. Add peas to pot. Cut roast into bite-sized pieces and return to pot. Stir stew and heat through.

BEEF AND MUSHROOM STEW

2-pound boneless beef roast

1 tsp. beef bouillon

1/4 cup all-purpose flour

3 Tbsp. Worcestershire sauce

1 tsp. Italian seasoning

1 4-oz. can mushrooms

1/2 pound baby carrots

1/2 onion, chopped

Place roast in crock pot and rub bouillon over top. Sprinkle flour over roast. Add remaining ingredients and 1 cup water. Sprinkle with salt and pepper if desired. Cook on high 4-5 hours or low 7-8 hours. Remove roast. Cut roast into bite-sized pieces and return to pot. Stir stew and heat through.

MUSHROOM CUBED STEAK

3 medium cubed steaks
1 tsp. beef bouillon
1 pound baby carrots
6 medium potatoes, peeled and chopped
1 onion, chopped
2 stalks celery, sliced (opt.)

Salt and pepper
1 family-sized cream
   of mushroom soup
1 cup sour cream
1 cup milk

Tenderize steaks with a meat mallet. Place cubed steaks in crock pot and sprinkle bouillon over top. Add remaining ingredients in order given. Cook on high 4-5 hours or low 7-8 hours. Cut steaks into smaller chunks before serving.

SMOTHERED PORK CHOPS

Follow recipe for Mushroom Cubed Steak, substituting six medium pork chops for the cubed steaks. When cooking time is done, carefully remove pork chops and place each one on an individual plate. Smother chops with vegetables and mushroom sauce.

ORANGE CHICKEN

6 boneless, skinless chicken breasts

2 tsp. chicken bouillon

1/3 cup teriyaki sauce

4 garlic cloves, minced

1 cup orange marmalade

2 cups water

6 green onions, chopped

3 Tbsp. cornstarch

3/4 cup walnuts, chopped

Place chicken breasts in crock pot and sprinkle with bouillon. Blend remaining ingredients except walnuts together and pour over chicken. Cook on high 4-5 hours or low 6-7 hours. Add walnuts and continue cooking while making White Steamed Rice to serve with chicken.

WHITE STEAMED RICE

4 cups water

2 cups white long-grain rice

2 Tbsp. butter

1 tsp. salt

Bring water to boil. Stir in butter and salt until butter melts. Add rice and stir well. Reduce heat to low and cover with tight-fitting lid. Simmer for 20 minutes. Remove from heat and allow to sit about 5 minutes. Fluff with fork.

CHICKEN AND WILD RICE

6 boneless, skinless chicken breasts

2 tsp. chicken bouillon

2 cups water

2 cans cream of chicken soup

4 large carrots, peeled and sliced

1 6-oz. pkg. seasoned
long-grain and wild rice mix

2 cups broccoli florets

Place chicken in crock pot and sprinkle with bouillon. Blend remaining ingredients except broccoli together and pour over chicken. Cook on high 4-5 hours or low 6-7 hours. Add broccoli during last hour of cooking time.

CHICKEN CACCIATORE

4 boneless, skinless chicken breasts

1 tsp. chicken bouillon

1 tsp. garlic powder

1 Tbsp. Italian seasoning

2 cans Italian-style diced tomatoes

1 large onion, chopped

1 4-oz. can mushrooms

Cooked spaghetti noodles

Place chicken breasts in crock pot and sprinkle with bouillon. Add remaining ingredients. Cook on high 4-5 hours or low for 6-7 hours. Remove chicken and cut each breast in half. Thicken sauce with 2 Tbsp. sugar and 2 Tbsp. cornstarch. Place each breast half on hot cooked noodles and smother with sauce.

CHICKEN AND DUMPLINGS

4 boneless, skinless chicken breasts

1 tsp. chicken bouillon

2 cups baby carrots

2 medium potatoes, peeled and chopped

2 stalks celery, sliced

1 medium onion, chopped

2 cans cream of chicken soup

1 can water

2 tsp. parsley flakes

1 tsp. poultry seasoning

Salt and pepper

Biscuit Topping

Place chicken in crock pot. Add remaining ingredients except Biscuit Topping in order given. Cook on high 4-5 hours or low 7-8 hours. Cut chicken into smaller pieces. Prepare Biscuit Topping and spoon over chicken mixture. Tilt lid to vent steam and cook on high for 30 minutes or until biscuits are cooked in the center.

Biscuit Topping:

2 cups all-purpose flour

4 tsp. baking powder

1 tsp. salt

2 Tbsp. sugar

Cut in until coarse and crumbly:

1/2 cup butter or shortening

Add and stir until completely moist:

2/3 cup cold milk

54

CREAMY CHICKEN AND NOODLES

4 boneless, skinless chicken breasts
1 tsp. chicken bouillon
6 carrots, peeled and sliced
1 onion, finely chopped
2 stalks celery, finely chopped
1 cup dairy sour cream
1 can cream of chicken soup
1/2 cup water
1 4-oz. can diced green chiles (opt.)
Hot cooked egg noodles
Parmesan cheese
Parsley flakes

Place chicken in crock pot and sprinkle with bouillon. Add remaining ingredients except noodles, cheese, and parsley. Cook on high 4-5 hours or low 7-8 hours. Cut chicken into smaller chunks. Serve over hot egg noodles and sprinkle with Parmesan cheese and parsley flakes.

TENDER TURKEY BREAST

4- to 5-pound turkey breast

1 tsp. poultry seasoning

1 Tbsp. parsley flakes

1 envelope turkey gravy mix

1 cup water

1 pkg. stuffing mix

Rinse turkey breast and pat dry. Rub with poultry seasoning. Place in crock pot and sprinkle parsley on top. Cook on high 4 hours or low 8 hours. Mix gravy and water and pour over turkey. Sprinkle stuffing mix on top. Cook additional hour on high or until meat thermometer reads 170 at center. Let stand 10 minutes before slicing. Serve with stuffing and choice of vegetables.

MARINATED TURKEY

2 pounds turkey breast meat

2 cups lemon-lime soft drink

1 cup vegetable oil

1 cup soy sauce

1/2 tsp. garlic powder

Cut turkey breast meat into bite-sized chunks. Mix remaining ingredients together in large bowl. Place turkey meat so it is covered with marinade. Cover with tight-fitting lid and refrigerate 24 hours. Shake bowl occasionally. Place turkey and 1 cup marinade in crock pot. Discard remaining marinade. Cook on high 3-4 hours, occasionally basting with marinade.

56

PERFECT POT ROAST

4- to 5-pound beef roast (of your choice)
1-2 tsp. beef bouillon or Kitchen Bouquet

Place roast in crock pot. Rub bouillon or Kitchen Bouquet on roast. (Note: You can also use au jus or beef gravy mix.) Cover and cook on high 4-5 hours or low 7-8 hours. Turn heat off and baste with juices. Allow to cool 10-15 minutes before slicing.

After a good dinner, one can forgive anybody, even one's own relative.
Oscar Wilde

ROAST AND VEGETABLES

4- to 5-pound beef roast
1-2 tsp. beef bouillon
1 pound baby carrots

6 potatoes, peeled and chopped
1 medium onion, chopped

Follow directions for Perfect Pot Roast, but place prepared vegetables in order given on top of roast before cooking. Remove vegetables carefully and place them around roast on serving tray, or serve them in a separate dish.

CHEESY HAM POTATOES

1 pound cooked ham, diced
6 potatoes, peeled and sliced
4 green onions, chopped
1 cup milk

1 can cream of chicken soup
1 cup dairy sour cream
1 cup cheddar cheese, grated
2 cups corn flakes, crushed

Place all ingredients except corn flakes in order given. Cook on high 4-5 hours or low 7-8 hours. Stir well. Saute corn flakes in 1 tablespoon butter, and sprinkle over potatoes. Cook additional 30 minutes with lid removed.

HAM HOCKS AND BEANS

1 ham bone with ham meat
2 cups dry small white beans
1/2 onion, chopped
2 tsp. garlic powder

1 tsp. black pepper
1 tsp. salt
2 quarts water

Place all ingredients in crock pot. Cook on high 5-6 hours or low 7-9 hours. Remove ham hock. Remove any ham still remaining on bone. Discard bone. Cut up any large pieces of ham and return to pot.

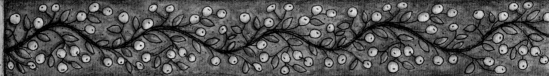

BEAN AND SAUSAGE STEW

1 pound sweet Italian sausage, browned
1 Tbsp. chicken bouillon
2 quarts water
2 medium carrots, peeled and chopped
1 stalk celery, chopped

1/2 cup dry pinto beans
1 cup dry navy beans
1/2 cup dry kidney beans
1 tsp. garlic powder
1 16-oz. can diced tomatoes

Cook sausage until browned. Place sausage and remaining ingredients except tomatoes in crock pot. Sprinkle with salt and pepper. Cook on high 4-5 hours or low 7-9 hours, until beans are tender. Add tomatoes and cook 30 minutes. If desired, sprinkle with Parmesan cheese.

CROCK POT CHILI BEANS

2 pounds hamburger, browned
1/2 onion, chopped
2 cups small red beans
1 pkg. chili seasoning mix

2 quarts water
1 can tomato sauce
1 cup salsa

Brown hamburger with salt, pepper, and garlic powder. Drain fat. Cook on high 4-6 hours or until beans are tender. Add tomato sauce and salsa. Cook additional 30 minutes. If desired, sprinkle with fresh chopped onions and grated cheese.

59

In the dessert section I mentioned that I don't remember having desserts except on holidays, but as I was compiling this section, I remembered the many times we had treats after family home evening. I can still see my brothers shaking the big heavy pot vigorously over the red-hot burner to pop the popcorn. Then they would dump it in a paper bag and we took turns shaking like crazy to get the butter and salt mixed in. I remember pulling taffy with my big sister, Julie. We stood opposite each other and pulled back as far as we could go and then brought our ends back, kind of like folding a blanket. We had to repeat the process a hundred times, but we loved it! My favorite treat was the date bars my mother used to bake. It wasn't very often, but when she did, the aroma filled the house, and we were all anxious for the lesson to be over so we could devour those wonderful treats!

This collection has been compiled with family home evening in mind. The pages are filled with fun and tasty recipes and ideas that children will love to make and eat. Some take time and others are simple, but I hope each one will create moments and special bonds that will be remembered for a very long time.

Family Night

Treats and Snacks

SOFT SUGAR COOKIES

1 1/4 cups butter, softened
1 1/2 cups granulated sugar
2 tsp. baking powder
1/2 tsp. salt
2 eggs

2 Tbsp. milk
2 tsp. vanilla
4 cups all-purpose flour
Powdered Sugar Frosting

Beat butter with electric mixer until smooth. Add sugar, baking powder, and salt. Beat until combined. Beat in eggs, milk, and vanilla until combined. Beat in as much flour as you can with mixer. Stir in any remaining flour. Divide dough in half. On a lightly floured surface, roll dough 1/4 inch thick. Cut dough into shapes. Place 1 inch apart on ungreased cookie sheet. Bake at 375 for 7-8 minutes or until edges are firm and bottoms are lightly browned. Place on wire rack and let cool. Frost if desired.

POWDERED SUGAR FROSTING

Beat 6 tablespoons butter until creamy. Add 1 tsp. vanilla and mix in. Gradually stir in powdered sugar (about 2 cups) until frosting is smooth and creamy.

62

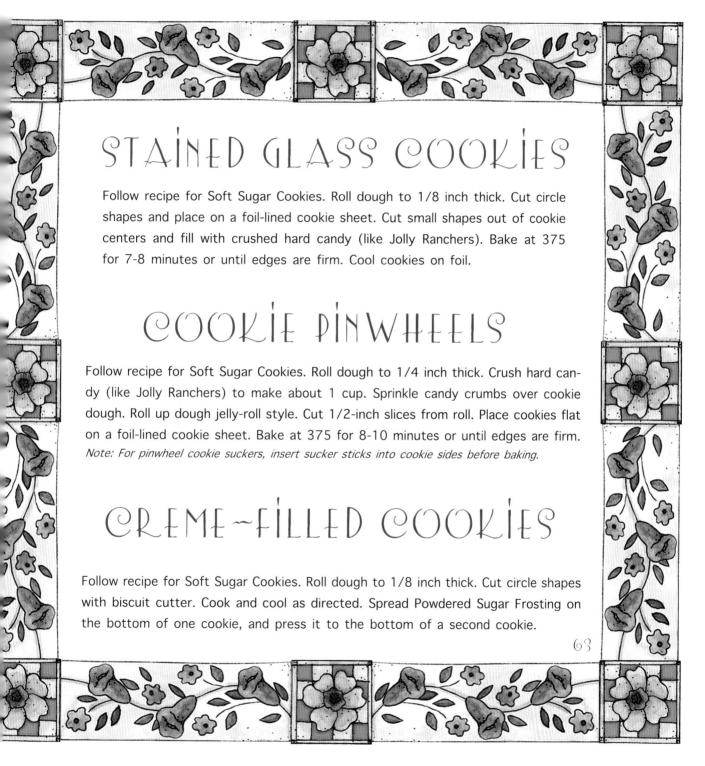

STAINED GLASS COOKIES

Follow recipe for Soft Sugar Cookies. Roll dough to 1/8 inch thick. Cut circle shapes and place on a foil-lined cookie sheet. Cut small shapes out of cookie centers and fill with crushed hard candy (like Jolly Ranchers). Bake at 375 for 7-8 minutes or until edges are firm. Cool cookies on foil.

COOKIE PINWHEELS

Follow recipe for Soft Sugar Cookies. Roll dough to 1/4 inch thick. Crush hard candy (like Jolly Ranchers) to make about 1 cup. Sprinkle candy crumbs over cookie dough. Roll up dough jelly-roll style. Cut 1/2-inch slices from roll. Place cookies flat on a foil-lined cookie sheet. Bake at 375 for 8-10 minutes or until edges are firm. *Note: For pinwheel cookie suckers, insert sucker sticks into cookie sides before baking.*

CREME~FILLED COOKIES

Follow recipe for Soft Sugar Cookies. Roll dough to 1/8 inch thick. Cut circle shapes with biscuit cutter. Cook and cool as directed. Spread Powdered Sugar Frosting on the bottom of one cookie, and press it to the bottom of a second cookie.

63

OATMEAL SANDWICH CREMES

1 cup butter, softened

3 cups brown sugar

4 eggs

2 tsp. cinnamon

Filling:

2 egg whites

2 tsp. vanilla

4 Tbsp. milk

1 1/2 tsp. nutmeg

1 tsp. baking soda

3 cups flour

3 cups quick oats

4 cups powdered sugar

1 cup butter, softened

Cream together butter, sugar, eggs, cinnamon, and nutmeg. Add remaining ingredients and mix well. Drop by tablespoonfuls onto greased cookie sheet. Flatten. Bake at 350 for 10-12 minutes. Do not overbake.

Filling: Beat egg whites. Add vanilla, milk, butter, and 2 cups powdered sugar. Beat thoroughly. Add remaining powdered sugar and mix well. Spread filling over one cookie and top with another cookie. Repeat.

FUDGE SANDWICH CREMES

Mix 1 box devil's food cake mix, 2 eggs, and 3/4 cup softened butter together. Drop by tablespoonfuls onto greased baking sheet. Bake at 350 for 10 minutes. Cookies will not look done, but remove from oven. Cool and fill as above.

64

GINGERBREAD FRIENDS

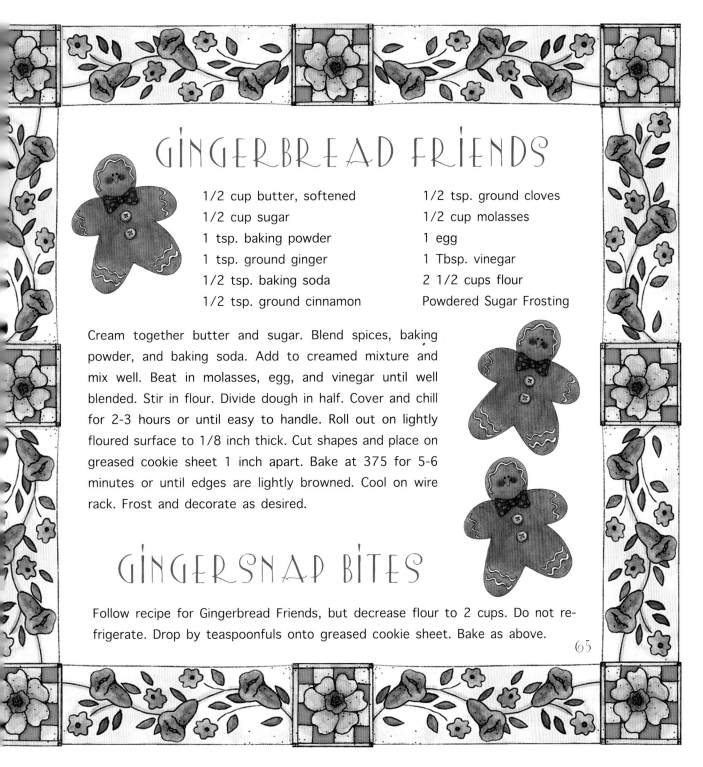

1/2 cup butter, softened
1/2 cup sugar
1 tsp. baking powder
1 tsp. ground ginger
1/2 tsp. baking soda
1/2 tsp. ground cinnamon

1/2 tsp. ground cloves
1/2 cup molasses
1 egg
1 Tbsp. vinegar
2 1/2 cups flour
Powdered Sugar Frosting

Cream together butter and sugar. Blend spices, baking powder, and baking soda. Add to creamed mixture and mix well. Beat in molasses, egg, and vinegar until well blended. Stir in flour. Divide dough in half. Cover and chill for 2-3 hours or until easy to handle. Roll out on lightly floured surface to 1/8 inch thick. Cut shapes and place on greased cookie sheet 1 inch apart. Bake at 375 for 5-6 minutes or until edges are lightly browned. Cool on wire rack. Frost and decorate as desired.

GINGERSNAP BITES

Follow recipe for Gingerbread Friends, but decrease flour to 2 cups. Do not re-frigerate. Drop by teaspoonfuls onto greased cookie sheet. Bake as above.

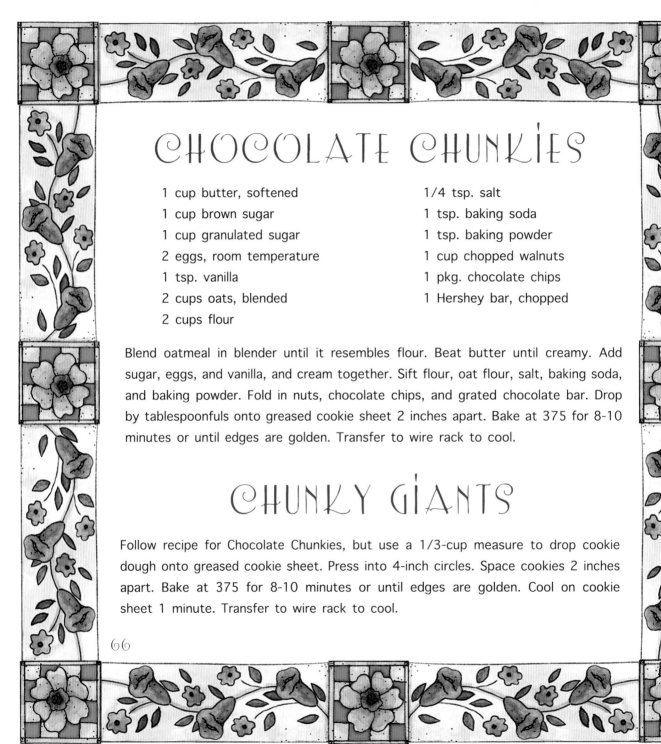

CHOCOLATE CHUNKIES

1 cup butter, softened
1 cup brown sugar
1 cup granulated sugar
2 eggs, room temperature
1 tsp. vanilla
2 cups oats, blended
2 cups flour

1/4 tsp. salt
1 tsp. baking soda
1 tsp. baking powder
1 cup chopped walnuts
1 pkg. chocolate chips
1 Hershey bar, chopped

Blend oatmeal in blender until it resembles flour. Beat butter until creamy. Add sugar, eggs, and vanilla, and cream together. Sift flour, oat flour, salt, baking soda, and baking powder. Fold in nuts, chocolate chips, and grated chocolate bar. Drop by tablespoonfuls onto greased cookie sheet 2 inches apart. Bake at 375 for 8-10 minutes or until edges are golden. Transfer to wire rack to cool.

CHUNKY GIANTS

Follow recipe for Chocolate Chunkies, but use a 1/3-cup measure to drop cookie dough onto greased cookie sheet. Press into 4-inch circles. Space cookies 2 inches apart. Bake at 375 for 8-10 minutes or until edges are golden. Cool on cookie sheet 1 minute. Transfer to wire rack to cool.

66

BEST BROWNIES EVER

1 cup butter	1/4 tsp. salt
1/2 cup cocoa powder	4 eggs
2 cups flour	2 cups sugar
1 tsp. baking powder	2 tsp. vanilla

Melt butter in saucepan. Remove from heat and stir in cocoa and sugar until well blended. Add eggs and stir just until blended. Do not over-stir. Sift flour, baking powder, and salt together. Add to cocoa mixture and stir well. Stir in vanilla. Pour into buttered 9x13 pan. Bake at 350 for 20-25 minutes or until edges look firm. Cool on wire rack.

BROWNIE FUDGE BITES

Follow recipe for Best Brownies Ever, but melt 1/3 cup chocolate chips with butter, reduce flour to 1 1/3 cups, and replace baking powder with 1/2 tsp. baking soda. Bake and cool as directed. Spread with Fudge Frosting and cut into bite-sized brownies.

Fudge Frosting: Stir 3/4 cup semisweet chocolate chips and 1/2 cup whipping cream together in saucepan. Cook and stir over low heat until chocolate is melted. Increase to medium heat and cook 3 minutes more, stirring continuously. Remove from heat and stir in 1/2 tsp. corn syrup. Chill until cool enough to spread.

NO~BAKE COOKIES

1/2 cup butter

1 1/2 cups sugar

1/4 cup cocoa powder

1/2 cup milk

1/2 cup peanut butter

1 tsp. vanilla

3 cups quick oats

Melt butter in medium saucepan. Add sugar and cocoa and mix well. Add milk and continue cooking and stirring over medium heat until mixture comes to a boil. Add peanut butter and stir until peanut butter melts. Remove from heat. Stir in vanilla and oats. Drop onto greased cookie sheet. Serve warm or cooled.

A boy (at any age) may think his mother can't relate to him and feel as though he doesn't have anything to say to her. But if the mother can persuade the boy to help her make a batch of cookies, somewhere during the mixing, or the baking, or the eating, he will open up and share his thoughts.

MUDDY NO~BAKE MOUNDS

Follow recipe for No-Bake Cookies. Remove from heat and stir in vanilla and oats as instructed, but also stir in 1/2 cup powdered sugar and 1/2 cup coconut. Continue as directed.

PEANUT BUTTER COOKIES

1 cup butter, softened	1 tsp. baking powder
1 cup peanut butter	2 eggs
1 cup sugar	1 tsp. vanilla
1 cup brown sugar	2 1/2 cups flour
1 tsp. baking soda	

Beat butter and peanut butter together until creamy. Cream in sugars, baking soda, and baking powder. Add eggs and vanilla and mix well. Stir in flour until well blended. Roll dough into 1-inch balls. Roll balls in granulated sugar and place on ungreased cookie sheet 2 inches apart. Flatten with tines of fork to make a crisscross. Bake at 375 for 7-9 minutes or until bottoms are lightly brown. Transfer to wire rack to cool.

PEANUT BUTTER KISSES

Follow recipe for Peanut Butter Cookies, but do not press with fork tines. Bake at 350 for 10-12 minutes or until edges are firm. Remove from oven and immediately press an unwrapped chocolate kiss into the center of each cookie. Transfer to wire rack to cool.

69

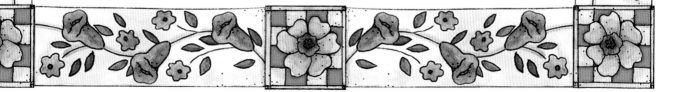

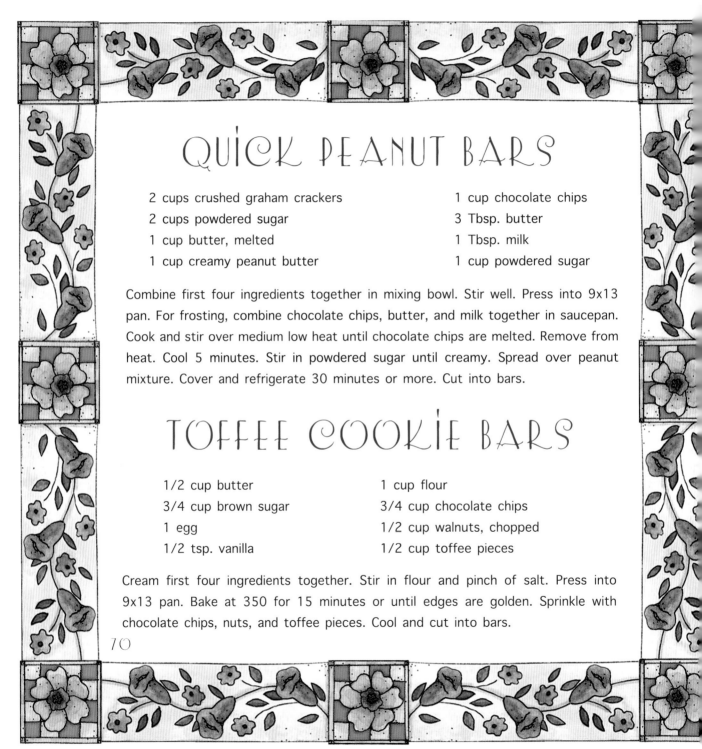

QUICK PEANUT BARS

2 cups crushed graham crackers

2 cups powdered sugar

1 cup butter, melted

1 cup creamy peanut butter

1 cup chocolate chips

3 Tbsp. butter

1 Tbsp. milk

1 cup powdered sugar

Combine first four ingredients together in mixing bowl. Stir well. Press into 9x13 pan. For frosting, combine chocolate chips, butter, and milk together in saucepan. Cook and stir over medium low heat until chocolate chips are melted. Remove from heat. Cool 5 minutes. Stir in powdered sugar until creamy. Spread over peanut mixture. Cover and refrigerate 30 minutes or more. Cut into bars.

TOFFEE COOKIE BARS

1/2 cup butter

3/4 cup brown sugar

1 egg

1/2 tsp. vanilla

1 cup flour

3/4 cup chocolate chips

1/2 cup walnuts, chopped

1/2 cup toffee pieces

Cream first four ingredients together. Stir in flour and pinch of salt. Press into 9x13 pan. Bake at 350 for 15 minutes or until edges are golden. Sprinkle with chocolate chips, nuts, and toffee pieces. Cool and cut into bars.

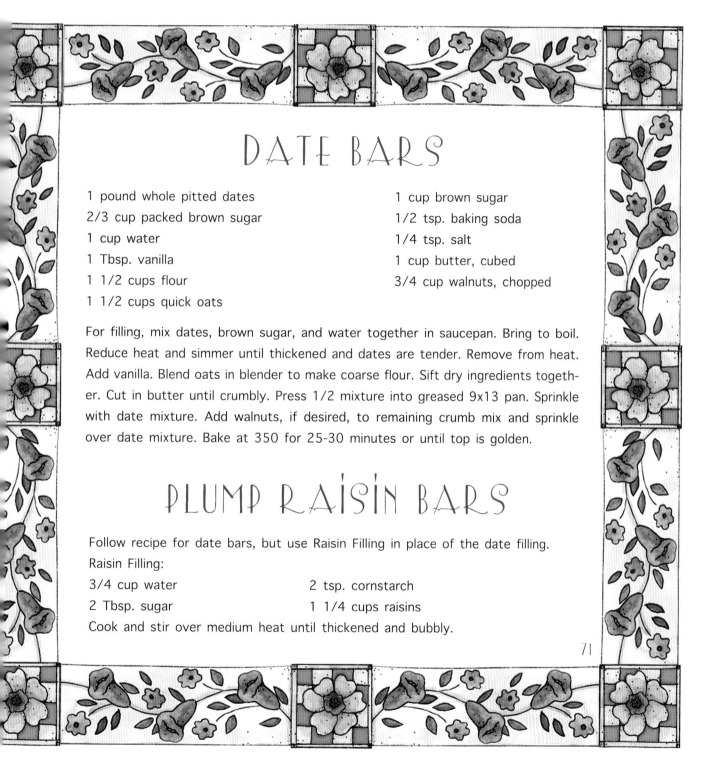

DATE BARS

1 pound whole pitted dates

2/3 cup packed brown sugar

1 cup water

1 Tbsp. vanilla

1 1/2 cups flour

1 1/2 cups quick oats

1 cup brown sugar

1/2 tsp. baking soda

1/4 tsp. salt

1 cup butter, cubed

3/4 cup walnuts, chopped

For filling, mix dates, brown sugar, and water together in saucepan. Bring to boil. Reduce heat and simmer until thickened and dates are tender. Remove from heat. Add vanilla. Blend oats in blender to make coarse flour. Sift dry ingredients together. Cut in butter until crumbly. Press 1/2 mixture into greased 9x13 pan. Sprinkle with date mixture. Add walnuts, if desired, to remaining crumb mix and sprinkle over date mixture. Bake at 350 for 25-30 minutes or until top is golden.

PLUMP RAISIN BARS

Follow recipe for date bars, but use Raisin Filling in place of the date filling.

Raisin Filling:

3/4 cup water

2 Tbsp. sugar

2 tsp. cornstarch

1 1/4 cups raisins

Cook and stir over medium heat until thickened and bubbly.

71

APRICOT BARS

1 1/2 cups butter, softened
1 1/2 cups sugar
3 eggs, well beaten

3 cups flour
3/4 cup apricot jam
2 Tbsp. sugar

Cream butter, sugar, and eggs. Add flour and mix thoroughly. Press half flour mixture into bottom of 9x13 pan. Spread jam over crust. Sprinkle remaining flour mixture over jam. Sprinkle with sugar. Bake at 350 for 30-40 minutes or until edges are golden brown.

RASPBERRY BARS

Follow recipe for Apricot Bars, but replace apricot jam with seedless raspberry jam.

And ye will not suffer your children that they ... fight and quarrel one with another... But ye will teach them to love one another, and to serve one another. . . .

Mosiah 4:14-15

72

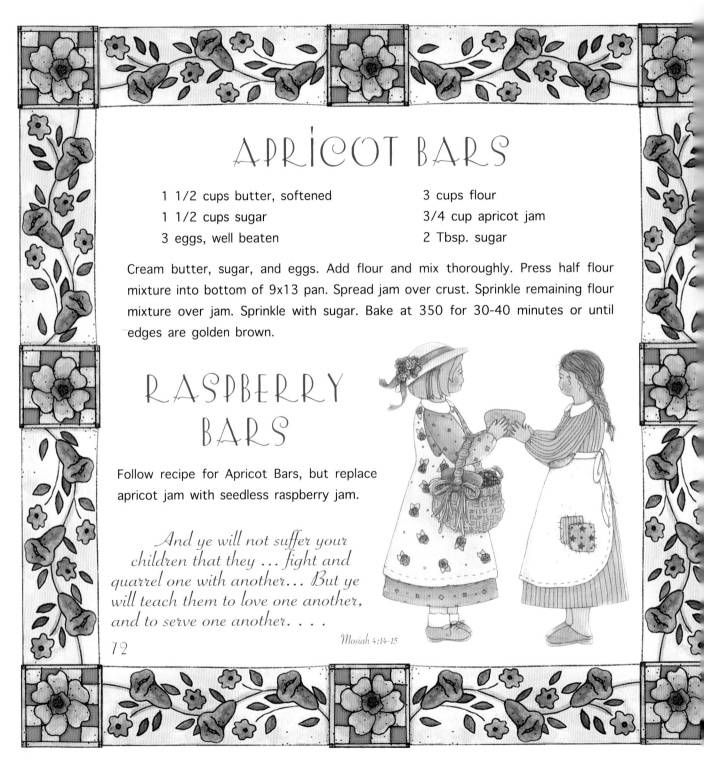

LEMON BARS

2 cups flour
1/2 cup powdered sugar
1/4 tsp. salt
3/4 cup sugar
3/4 cup butter

4 eggs, slightly beaten
1 1/2 cups sugar
1/4 cup flour
1/2 cup lemon juice
Powdered sugar

Blend first four ingredients. Press 2/3 mixture into 9x13 pan. Bake at 350 for 15 minutes. Whisk eggs, sugar, flour, and lemon juice together. Pour over crust. Bake additional 15-20 minutes or until center is set. Cool. Sprinkle with powdered sugar.

CHEESECAKE BARS

1/2 cup flour
1/2 cup walnuts, finely chopped
1/2 cup flaked coconut
1/4 cup butter
2 8-oz. pkgs. cream cheese

1/2 cup sugar
2 eggs
1 tsp. vanilla
1 21-oz. can pie filling

Combine first four ingredients. Press 2/3 mixture into 9x13 pan. Bake at 350 for 15 minutes. Beat sugar, cream cheese, egg, and vanilla together. Spread over crust and bake 15 minutes. Cool 10 minutes. Spread pie filling on top and sprinkle with remaining crumb mixture. Bake 30 minutes. Cool and cut into bars.

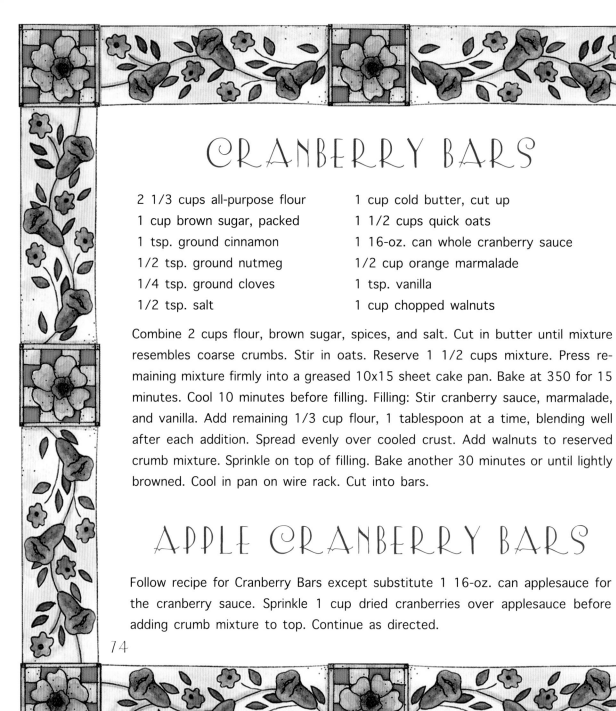

CRANBERRY BARS

2 1/3 cups all-purpose flour

1 cup brown sugar, packed

1 tsp. ground cinnamon

1/2 tsp. ground nutmeg

1/4 tsp. ground cloves

1/2 tsp. salt

1 cup cold butter, cut up

1 1/2 cups quick oats

1 16-oz. can whole cranberry sauce

1/2 cup orange marmalade

1 tsp. vanilla

1 cup chopped walnuts

Combine 2 cups flour, brown sugar, spices, and salt. Cut in butter until mixture resembles coarse crumbs. Stir in oats. Reserve 1 1/2 cups mixture. Press remaining mixture firmly into a greased 10x15 sheet cake pan. Bake at 350 for 15 minutes. Cool 10 minutes before filling. Filling: Stir cranberry sauce, marmalade, and vanilla. Add remaining 1/3 cup flour, 1 tablespoon at a time, blending well after each addition. Spread evenly over cooled crust. Add walnuts to reserved crumb mixture. Sprinkle on top of filling. Bake another 30 minutes or until lightly browned. Cool in pan on wire rack. Cut into bars.

APPLE CRANBERRY BARS

Follow recipe for Cranberry Bars except substitute 1 16-oz. can applesauce for the cranberry sauce. Sprinkle 1 cup dried cranberries over applesauce before adding crumb mixture to top. Continue as directed.

74

BAKED APPLE TARTS

2 1/2 cups flour	3 Tbsp. flour
1 tsp. salt	3 Tbsp. brown sugar
2 Tbsp. sugar	1/8 tsp. nutmeg
1 cup butter	1/8 tsp. cinnamon
6 apples, cored	2 tbsp. butter

Sift flour, salt, and sugar together. Cut in butter until coarse and crumbly. While stirring, slowly add 4-6 tablespoons of water until dough forms a ball. Roll dough on lightly floured surface into a 12x18 rectangle. Cut six 6-inch squares. Place one cored apple at center of each square. Combine last five ingredients together. Spoon 1 tablespoon mixture into center of each apple. Pull corners of dough to top of apple and pinch together to secure. If desired, push a cinnamon stick down through dough and apple. Place apples on greased baking sheet. Bake at 375 for 45 minutes. Remove from oven and brush crusts with milk. Sprinkle with cinnamon and sugar. Return to oven and bake 15 minutes more. Serve warm.

CARAMEL APPLES

8 Granny Smith apples - 8 sticks - 1 Caramels recipe

Insert sticks into apples. Make Caramels. Butter a large cookie sheet. Dip apples into caramel and place apples on cookie sheet. Allow to cool before serving.

CARAMELS

2 cups granulated sugar

1 cup brown sugar

1 cup light corn syrup

1 cup heavy cream

1 cup milk

1 cup butter

1 1/4 tsp. vanilla

In a saucepan combine all ingredients except vanilla. Cook and stir over medium-high heat until candy boils. Continue cooking, stirring frequently until candy reaches firm-ball stage (248 degrees, or when a small amount of candy dropped into cold water makes a firm ball). Remove from heat and stir in vanilla. Pour into greased 9-inch square baking pan. Cool. When firm, cut into squares and individually wrap in waxed paper or plastic wrap.

ENGLISH TOFFEE

1 cup butter

1 cup sugar

1/4 cup water

1 tsp. vanilla

1 6-oz. pkg. chocolate chips

1/2 cup walnuts, finely chopped

Combine butter, sugar, and water in a saucepan. Over medium heat bring to hard-crack stage (300 degrees), stirring occasionally (takes about 30 minutes). Remove from heat and stir in vanilla. Pour onto ungreased baking sheet while still hot. Sprinkle with chocolate chips, and spread when they melt. Sprinkle with chopped walnuts. Cool completely and break into pieces.

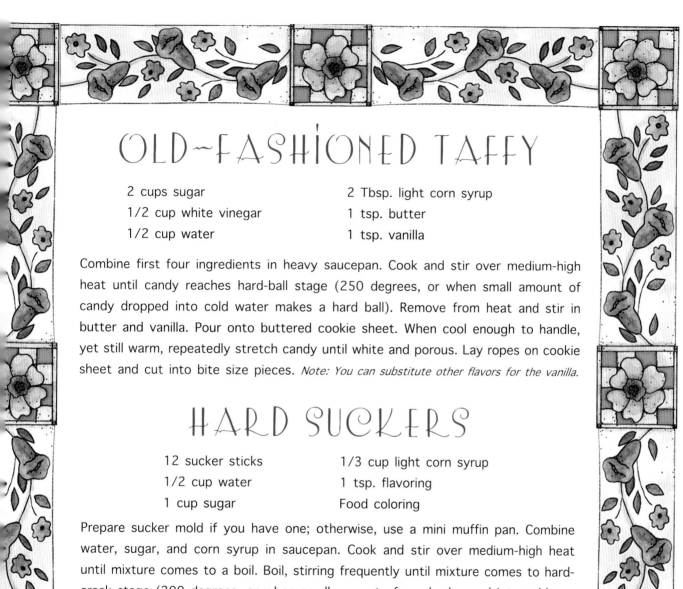

OLD~FASHIONED TAFFY

2 cups sugar

1/2 cup white vinegar

1/2 cup water

2 Tbsp. light corn syrup

1 tsp. butter

1 tsp. vanilla

Combine first four ingredients in heavy saucepan. Cook and stir over medium-high heat until candy reaches hard-ball stage (250 degrees, or when small amount of candy dropped into cold water makes a hard ball). Remove from heat and stir in butter and vanilla. Pour onto buttered cookie sheet. When cool enough to handle, yet still warm, repeatedly stretch candy until white and porous. Lay ropes on cookie sheet and cut into bite size pieces. *Note: You can substitute other flavors for the vanilla.*

HARD SUCKERS

12 sucker sticks

1/2 cup water

1 cup sugar

1/3 cup light corn syrup

1 tsp. flavoring

Food coloring

Prepare sucker mold if you have one; otherwise, use a mini muffin pan. Combine water, sugar, and corn syrup in saucepan. Cook and stir over medium-high heat until mixture comes to a boil. Boil, stirring frequently until mixture comes to hard-crack stage (300 degrees, or when small amount of candy dropped into cold water turns brittle). Remove from heat. Stir in flavoring and food coloring. Pour into molds and put sticks in place. Allow to cool.

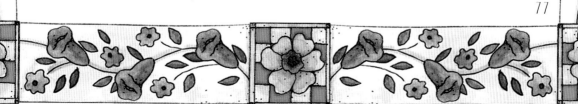

FRUITY POPCORN BALLS

- 10 cups popped popcorn
- 2 6-oz. pkgs. fruit gelatin
  (any flavor)
- 1 cup butter

- 1/2 cup light corn syrup
- 1 tsp. vanilla

Remove unpopped kernels from popcorn. Butter 2 large bowls and divide popped corn into bowls. Combine gelatin, butter, and corn syrup in saucepan. Cook and stir over medium heat until mixture comes to a boil. Boil without stirring for 3 minutes. Remove from heat and stir in vanilla. Pour gelatin mixture over popcorn and stir with wooden spoon to coat popcorn. Butter hands and shape popcorn into balls.

SOFT CARAMEL POPCORN

- 6 cups popped popcorn
- 1 cup brown sugar
- 1/2 cup butter

- 1/4 cup light corn syrup
- 1 tsp. vanilla

Remove unpopped corn kernels from popcorn. Dump popcorn into large buttered bowl. Combine brown sugar, butter, and corn syrup in saucepan. Cook and stir over medium heat until mixture comes to a boil. Boil without stirring for 3 minutes. Remove from heat and stir in vanilla. Pour caramel over popcorn and stir with wooden spoon to coat popcorn. If desired, form into balls.

78

PAPER BAG POPCORN

1 cup unpopped popcorn
6 Tbsp. butter

Salt for seasoning
Large paper bag

Melt butter in saucepan. Using a hot air popper, pop the popcorn 1/2 cup at a time. Remove unpopped kernels. Dump popcorn into large paper grocery bag. Sprinkle about 1/2 tsp. salt (to taste) over popcorn. Pour hot butter over popcorn and begin shaking immediately. Shake until popcorn is well coated. Share popcorn right out of the bag.

TRAIL~MIX POPCORN

Follow recipe for Paper Bag Popcorn, but add 2 cups of your favorite trail mix, M&Ms, or other candies to buttered, salted popcorn. Shake well and serve while still warm.

SWEET HOT KETTLE CORN

1/3 cup vegetable oil   1/2 cup sugar   1/2 cup unpopped corn

Heat oil and sugar in heavy pot that has a tight-fitting lid. Stir in popcorn to coat well. Cover with lid and shake rapidly over medium heat until corn stops popping. Remove from heat and pour into large bowl. Lightly salt. Serve immediately.

ICE CREAM SANDWICHES

1 Best Brownies Ever recipe (unbaked)
1 2-quart carton ice cream, softened only until it can be cut

Grease and line 10x15 sheet cake pan and line with waxed paper. Make Best Brownies Ever batter according to recipe. Pour batter into prepared pan. Bake at 400 for 20 minutes, or until knife inserted near center comes out clean. Cool 10-15 minutes. Remove from pan and cool completely on wire rack. Cut brownie in half widthwise. Remove carton from ice cream. Cut ice cream widthwise into 1/2-inch thick slices. Place ice cream slices on one layer of brownie until completely covered. Place second brownie layer on top. Cut into individual bars. Wrap tightly with foil and freeze until ready to eat.

CANDY~COVERED ICE CREAM SANDWICHES

Ice Cream Sandwiches (above)
1 bottle hard-shell ice cream topping
1 cup broken candy bar pieces
Nuts or toppings of choice

Dip ice cream sandwiches into topping. Sprinkle with candy bar pieces, nuts, or other toppings of choice. Wrap tightly with foil and freeze.

80

BAGGY ICE CREAM

4 cups milk

2 cups whipping cream

2 1/2 cups powdered sugar

1 Tbsp. vanilla

1 bag crushed ice

Rock salt (opt.)

Zip-top sandwich bags

Zip-top gallon freezer bags

Stir first four ingredients together in mixing bowl until sugar dissolves. Measure 3/4 cup cream into sandwich bags and close tight. Fill freezer bag 1/3 full with crushed ice. Add 1/4 cup rock salt (optional; helps ice melt faster). Place closed sandwich bag inside freezer bag and close tight. Shake bag until cream freezes.

Note: You can also use a #10 can with a tight-fitting lid for this recipe. Fill can 1/3 full with crushed ice. Add 1/2 cup rock salt. Measure 2 cups cream mixture into gallon freezer bag, close tightly, and place in can. Replace lid and roll back and forth until ice cream freezes.

POPSICLE CUPS

2 envelopes punch powder

2 cups sugar

4 cups water

12 Popsicle sticks

Combine punch, sugar, and water in a pitcher. Stir until sugar is well dissolved. Pour 1/3 cup punch into each cup of cupcake pan. Freeze 1 hour or until punch is frozen enough to hold stick upright. Remove from freezer and place sticks in centers. Return to freezer. Freeze 2-3 hours or until completely frozen.

HOT FUDGE TOPPING

1 cup chocolate chips

1 cup whipping cream

1/2 tsp. vanilla

In a medium saucepan, combine chocolate chips and whipping cream. Cook and stir over medium heat until chocolate is completely melted and mixture thickens. Remove from heat and stir in vanilla. Serve over ice cream.

Note: You can substitute canned milk for the whipping cream.

CARAMEL TOPPING

2 Tbsp. butter

1 cup brown sugar, packed

1 cup whipping cream

1 tsp. vanilla

In a medium saucepan, melt butter. Stir in brown sugar and whipping cream. Cook and stir over medium heat until mixture boils. Cook an additional 1-2 minutes until mixture is thickened. Remove from heat. Stir in vanilla. Serve over ice cream.

Note: You can substitute canned milk for the whipping cream.

82

NUTTY BUDDIES

1 quart vanilla ice cream
1 recipe Hot Fudge Topping

1 cup chopped peanuts
8 Popsicle sticks

Cut the ice cream into eight equal squares. Push a Popsicle stick into each square of ice cream (so each resembles a sucker). Dip each square of ice cream into the hot fudge topping, then immediately roll in chopped peanuts. Place top side down on a tray, and freeze until ready to serve.

DRIVE~IN MILKSHAKES

1 cup milk
1 cup + more vanilla ice cream

1/4 cup chocolate syrup

Pour milk into blender. Slowly add ice cream and topping, blending until mixture becomes thick. You must add the ice cream slowly to prevent the milk from freezing. If you add too much ice cream at once, the ice cream will freeze the milk, resulting in ice crystals.
Note: You can substitute caramel topping, freezer jam (strawberry or raspberry), or other toppings of your choice for the chocolate syrup.

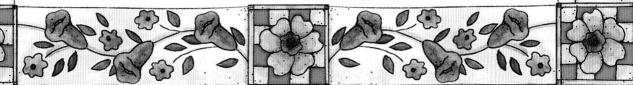

FRUIT PIZZA

Using the Soft Sugar Cookies recipe, roll dough 1/4 inch thick in shape to fit pizza pan. Place on ungreased pizza pan and bake at 375 for 10-12 minutes or until edges are firm and bottom is lightly browned. Cool on wire rack. Frost with Orange Cream Cheese Frosting and top with fruit of choice (sliced strawberries, kiwi fruit, mandarin oranges, peaches, etc.).

Orange Cream Cheese Frosting:

1 8-oz. pkg. cream cheese

3 Tbsp. orange juice concentrate

3 cups powdered sugar

Beat cream cheese until smooth. Add butter and orange juice. Cream together. Stir in enough powdered sugar to make a frosting that is easy to spread.

FRUITY FACES

Make large cookies using the Soft Sugar Cookies recipe. Frost cookies with Orange Cream Cheese Frosting (above).
Let children make faces on cookies using fresh, dried, or canned fruit.

84

FRESH FRUIT SALSA

2 cups strawberries, finely diced

1 cup peaches, finely diced

3 kiwi fruit, finely diced

1 4-oz. can mandarin oranges,
    drained and finely diced

2 bananas, finely diced

1 tsp. lemon juice

1/4 cup sugar

1/3 cup frozen orange
    juice concentrate

Combine all ingredients together in a mixing bowl. Allow to sit 30 minutes for flavors to blend before serving. Stir well and put in serving bowl. Serve with Cinnamon Chips.

When bringing up children, spend on them half as much money and twice as much time.

Unknown

CINNAMON CHIPS

10 flour tortillas

3/4 cup sugar

1 Tbsp. cinnamon

Butter to spread

Spread butter on tortillas. Place a few tortillas butter-side-up on cookie sheet. Blend sugar and cinnamon. Sprinkle tortillas with cinnamon-sugar mixture (if you have a shaker, use it). Broil 5 minutes or until tops start to bubble and turn golden brown. Remove from oven. Using a pizza cutter, slice tortillas into chips. Repeat cooking and cutting with remaining tortillas.

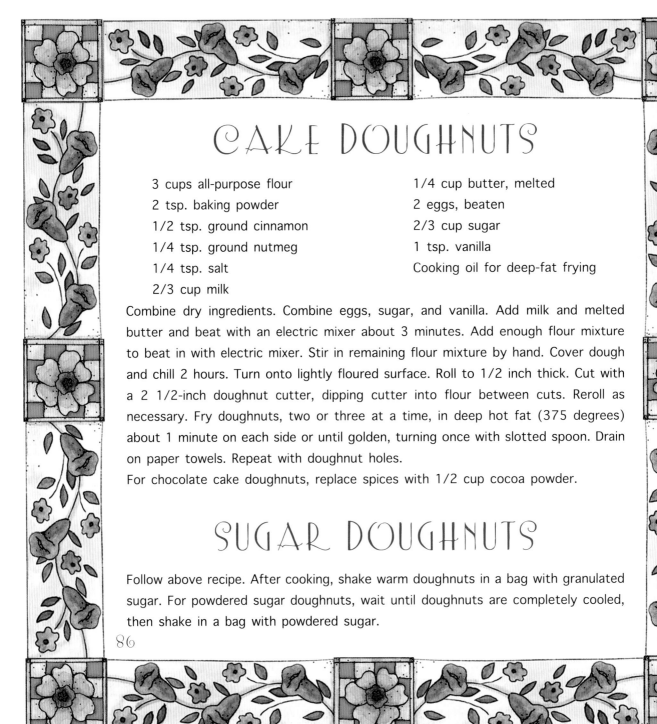

CAKE DOUGHNUTS

3 cups all-purpose flour
2 tsp. baking powder
1/2 tsp. ground cinnamon
1/4 tsp. ground nutmeg
1/4 tsp. salt
2/3 cup milk

1/4 cup butter, melted
2 eggs, beaten
2/3 cup sugar
1 tsp. vanilla
Cooking oil for deep-fat frying

Combine dry ingredients. Combine eggs, sugar, and vanilla. Add milk and melted butter and beat with an electric mixer about 3 minutes. Add enough flour mixture to beat in with electric mixer. Stir in remaining flour mixture by hand. Cover dough and chill 2 hours. Turn onto lightly floured surface. Roll to 1/2 inch thick. Cut with a 2 1/2-inch doughnut cutter, dipping cutter into flour between cuts. Reroll as necessary. Fry doughnuts, two or three at a time, in deep hot fat (375 degrees) about 1 minute on each side or until golden, turning once with slotted spoon. Drain on paper towels. Repeat with doughnut holes.

For chocolate cake doughnuts, replace spices with 1/2 cup cocoa powder.

SUGAR DOUGHNUTS

Follow above recipe. After cooking, shake warm doughnuts in a bag with granulated sugar. For powdered sugar doughnuts, wait until doughnuts are completely cooled, then shake in a bag with powdered sugar.

86

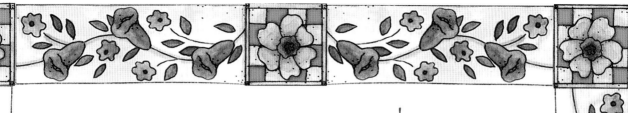

HOT COCOA MIX

3 cups sugar	3/4 tsp. salt
2 cups cocoa	9 cups powdered milk

Combine in air-tight container and store until ready to use. To make hot cocoa, mix 1 cup hot water with 1/3 cup cocoa mix.

MINT HOT COCOA

Pour hot cocoa in mug and stir with candy cane.

SPICED CIDER

8 cups apple cider or apple juice	1 tsp. whole cloves
1/4 cup packed brown sugar	1 tsp. shredded orange peel
6 inches stick cinnamon	1 tsp. whole allspice

In a large saucepan combine cider and sugar. Make a spice bag from a double-thick, 6-inch square of 100 percent cotton cheesecloth. Place cinnamon, allspice, cloves, and orange peel in center of cloth. Tie closed with a clean string. Add to cider. Bring to boil. Reduce heat. Cover and simmer 10 minutes. Serve hot.

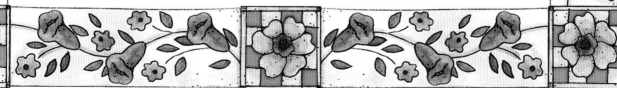

TRADITIONAL EGGNOG

8 egg yolks
1 cup sugar
5 cups milk

3 cups whipping cream
1 tsp. nutmeg
1 tsp. vanilla

Combine egg yolks, milk, and sugar in a saucepan. Cook and stir over medium heat until mixture coats a metal spoon. Remove from heat and cool in pan of ice water. Stir for 2 minutes. Add whipping cream, nutmeg, and vanilla. Stir well. Chill 4 to 24 hours in refrigerator.

For eggnog shakes, blend 1 cup eggnog and 1 cup ice cream in blender until creamy. Add more ice cream to desired thickness.

ORANGE JULIUS

1/2 cup orange juice concentrate
2 cups milk
1/3 cup sugar

1 tsp. vanilla
crushed ice cubes

Blend first four ingredients in blender. To crush ice cubes, place ice cubes in plastic bag and then in paper bag. Gently pound with side of rolling pin. Add crushed ice to mixture and blend. Continue adding ice until mixture reaches desired thickness.

88

FRUIT SMOOTHIES

2 cups milk

1/4 cup sugar

1-2 cups frozen fruit

1 tsp. vanilla

In blender combine milk, sugar, vanilla, and 1/4 cup of frozen fruit. Blend. Add 1/4 cup frozen fruit at a time until smoothie reaches desired thickness. Some of our favorite fruit smoothies are:

Apricot	Peach-Banana
Banana	Strawberry-Apricot
Peach	Strawberry-Banana
Strawberry	Stawberry-Peach

TIGER'S MILK SMOOTHIE

Follow recipe for Fruit Smoothies, using apricots for your frozen fruit. Add 2 tablespoons Brewer's yeast and blend until smooth.

Note: Don't tell your kids, but this drink is very high in vitamin B.

FRUIT SLUSHIES

Combine 1 cup fresh fruit, 1/2 cup sugar, and 1 cup ice in blender. Continue to blend in ice until slushy reaches desired consistency.

89

My daughter once told me that she learned in psychology that wherever the mother goes in the home, the children will follow (just like baby ducks!). I noticed that as I prepared meals, my children gathered in the kitchen, and before long they were helping and talking about their day. At dinner time, the ice had already been broken, and conversation was easy. This continued while we cleaned up, and as the family migrated into the living room, discussions grew deeper. We often talked about important things. Studies show that children and teens who eat dinner with their families at least five times a week are half as likely to use drugs or alcohol (www.ParentsEmpowered.org). I wasn't surprised when I saw that statistic, because I had already witnessed it in my own home.

I hope this collection of pasta and rice recipes will encourage your family to stay HOME for dinner!

Tuesday
Pasta and Rice

FETTUCCINE ALFREDO

3 Tbsp. butter
3 Tbsp. flour
2 cups milk
1/2 tsp. salt

1 tsp. garlic powder
1 cup whipping cream
1/4 cup Parmesan cheese
Cooked fettuccine noodles

Melt butter. Stir flour into butter while cooking until a smooth paste forms. Slowly stir in milk. Cook and stir over medium heat until thickened and bubbly. Add salt, garlic powder, and cream, and stir well. Stir in Parmesan cheese. Serve over hot cooked fettuccine noodles.

CHICKEN FETTUCCINE

2 boneless, skinless chicken
    breast halves
1 cup water

1 tsp. chicken bouillon
1/4 tsp. paprika
Alfredo sauce (recipe above)

Place chicken in water in medium saucepan. Sprinkle paprika and bouillon over top. Cover with lid and cook over medium-low heat 20-30 minutes until chicken is cooked and tender. Cut chicken apart while still in pan. This allows chicken to absorb the broth. Mix chicken and broth with Alfredo sauce. Serve over hot cooked fettuccine noodles.

92

SAUTEED ONION LINGUINE

4 Tbsp. butter

3 Tbsp. flour

1/2 onion, finely diced

1 stalk celery, finely diced

2 cups milk

1 tsp. garlic powder

1/2 tsp. salt

1 cup whipping cream

1/4 cup Parmesan cheese

Hot cooked linguine noodles

Melt butter. Saute onions and celery until onions start to brown. Stir flour into butter and onions until a smooth paste forms. Slowly stir in milk. Cook and stir over medium heat until thickened and bubbly. Add salt, garlic powder, and cream, and continue cooking and stirring until thickened and bubbly. Stir in Parmesan cheese. Serve over hot cooked linguine or fettuccini noodles.

SEAFOOD SAUCE AND PASTA

Follow above recipe for onion sauce, but add 4 green onions, chopped. (Do not saute the onions.) Add 1 6 1/2-oz. can minced clams, undrained, to the milk, garlic powder, and salt. Cook as directed. Serve over hot cooked linguine, spaghetti, or fettuccine noodles.

93

MEATY SPAGHETTI SAUCE

2 pounds sweet Italian sausage
2 pounds ground beef
8 garlic cloves, pressed
1/3 cup sugar

3 Tbsp. Italian seasoning
2 16-oz. cans tomato sauce
2 30-oz. cans crushed tomatoes
2 4-oz. cans mushrooms (opt.)

Brown meats together in a large soup pot, seasoning with salt, pepper, and garlic powder. Drain fat. Clean outer skin off garlic and break apart until you have 8 smaller cloves. Press cloves between two spoons or use garlic press. Add to meat along with remaining ingredients. Simmer, without a lid, on low 4-5 hours, stirring occasionally and skimming off fat as it surfaces. After sauce has cooked for a few hours, the garlic will soften. Press cloves again to break apart, and stir well into the sauce. Add additional seasonings or sugar to suit your taste. This recipe makes about 4 1/2 quarts of sauce. Serve over hot cooked spaghetti noodles or use in your favorite recipes.

QUICK MARINARA SAUCE

Stir 3 Tbsp. sugar, 2 tsp. Italian seasoning, and 1/2 tsp. garlic powder into 1 30-oz. can crushed tomatoes. Cook over medium heat 5 minutes.

94

OVEN~BAKED LASAGNA

12 lasagna noodles, cooked and drained

1 16-oz. carton cottage cheese

1 16-oz. carton ricotta cheese

2 cups grated mozzarella cheese

Parmesan cheese

1 Tbsp. parsley flakes

2 eggs

1 quart spaghetti sauce

Place cooked lasagna noodles individually on foil to prevent from sticking. Mix cottage and ricotta cheese, 1 1/2 cups mozzarella cheese, 1/4 cup Parmesan cheese, and parsley flakes together in a bowl. In a 9x13 baking pan, spread spaghetti sauce to cover bottom of pan. Using three noodles, place a layer of noodles over sauce and spread 1/3 cheese mixture on noodles. Spread sauce over cheese and repeat layers twice. Top with remaining noodles, sauce, and mozzarella cheese, and sprinkle with Parmesan cheese. Bake at 350 for 30-40 minutes or until cheese is melted and bubbly.

MEATY BAKED LASAGNA

Brown 2 pounds ground beef with salt, pepper, and garlic powder. Drain fat. Follow above recipe, spreading 1/3 of meat mixture on top of each layer of cheese mixture. Top with a layer of noodles, sauce, and cheese as directed above.

95

EASY CHICKEN PARMESAN

6 boneless, skinless chicken breast halves

1/2 cup fine bread crumbs

1/4 cup Parmesan cheese

2 Tbsp. parsley flakes

2 tsp. garlic powder

2 eggs, well beaten

1 1/2 quarts marinara sauce

2 cups mozzarella cheese

Mix bread crumbs, Parmesan cheese, parsley, and garlic in a bowl. Beat eggs together in a separate dish. Dip chicken in eggs and then in crumb mixture. Place chicken in greased 9x13 baking pan. Bake at 350 for 1 hour. Remove from oven and pour marinara sauce over chicken. Sprinkle with mozzarella cheese. Bake 30 minutes.

ZUCCHINI CHICKEN PARMESAN

Follow above recipe, but while chicken is baking, slice 2 medium zucchini and chop 1/2 onion. Steam together with a little salt and pepper, just until crisp-tender. Do not overcook. Drain well. Place zucchini on baked chicken before pouring marinara sauce on top. Continue as directed.

STUFFED MANICOTTI

1 12-oz. pkg. manicotti shells

1 16-oz. carton cottage cheese

1 16-oz. carton ricotta cheese

2 cups mozzarella cheese, grated

1/2 cup Parmesan cheese

2 eggs, well beaten

1 Tbsp. parsley flakes

1 quart spaghetti sauce

Cook manicotti according to package directions. Drain. Mix together the cheeses, eggs, and parsley in a bowl. In a 9x13 baking pan, spread sauce to cover bottom of pan. Fill each shell with cheese mixture until it spills out both ends. Place shell in baking pan. Top with sauce and sprinkle with mozzarella and Parmesan cheeses. Bake at 350 for 30-40 minutes or until cheese is melted.

CHEESE~STUFFED SHELLS

Follow above recipe, substituting jumbo shells for the manicotti shells. Cook jumbo shells according to package directions. Stuff shells with cheese mixture and place in baking pan. Spread sauce over shells and repeat with layer of stuffed shells. Cover with sauce and mozzarella and Parmesan cheese. Bake as above.

HAM AND CHEESE PENNE

3 cups penne pasta	1/4 tsp. ground black pepper
3 Tbsp. butter	1 cup whipping cream
3 Tbsp. flour	1 pound cooked ham, cubed
1 cup milk	2 cups mozzarella cheese, grated
1/2 tsp. paprika	1/2 cup Parmesan cheese
1/2 tsp. salt	1/2 cup garlic bread crumbs (opt.)

Cook penne according to package directions. Melt butter. Stir flour into butter while cooking until a smooth paste forms. Slowly stir in milk. Cook and stir over medium heat until thickened and bubbly. Add paprika, salt, pepper, and cream, and continue cooking and stirring until thickened. Stir in ham, mozzarella cheese, and penne. Turn into greased baking dish. Sprinkle with Parmesan cheese and bread crumbs (if desired). Broil for 5 minutes or until bread crumbs start to turn golden brown.

TOMATO BASIL PENNE

Follow above recipe, replacing the paprika with basil and replacing the ham with 3-4 roma or plum tomatoes, chopped.

GARLIC CHICKEN

12-oz. wide egg noodles

3 Tbsp. olive or vegetable oil

1 pound chicken, cut into 1-inch strips

2 garlic cloves, minced

1/4 cup water

4 green onions, chopped

1 Tbsp. butter

1/2 cup Parmesan cheese

Cook noodles according to package directions. While noodles are cooking, heat oil. Stir-fry chicken in oil until it turns white. Add garlic and green onions and continue stir-frying 3-4 minutes. Reduce temperature and add water. Allow chicken to steam until noodles are ready. Drain noodles. Dot with butter and sprinkle with salt. Fold noodles into chicken mix. Stir in Parmesan cheese.

TOMATO MACARONI BAKE

3 cups macaroni, cooked and drained

1 30-oz. can stewed tomatoes

1 16-oz. can whole-kernel corn, drained

2 cups cheddar cheese, grated

Salt and pepper to taste

Cook macaroni according to package directions. Drain and turn into greased 9x13 dish. Add remaining ingredients and stir well. Bake at 425 for 25-30 minutes.

DELUXE BEEF STROGANOFF

1 1/2 pounds beef stew meat

3 Tbsp. vegetable oil

1/2 cup flour

Salt and pepper

1 tsp. garlic powder

1 medium onion, chopped

1 cup mushrooms, sliced

2 tsp. beef bouillon

1 cup milk

2 tsp. Worcestershire sauce

1 cup whipping cream

Hot cooked egg noodles

Heat oil in a large skillet. Blend flour and seasonings in a large bag. Toss beef in flour mixture to coat well. Cook meat, onions, and mushrooms in hot oil until onions begin to turn clear. Dissolve bouillon in 1 cup water. Blend remaining flour mixture with water. Add to beef and onions and cook and stir over medium heat until a smooth paste forms. Slowly stir in milk and cook over medium heat until thickened and bubbly. Add Worcestershire sauce and cream (you can substitute canned milk) and continue cooking until thickened. Serve over hot cooked egg noodles.

The strength of a nation derives from the integrity of the home.

Confucius

100

EASY BEEF STROGANOFF

2 pounds ground beef, browned

1/2 onion, finely diced (opt.)

1 4-oz. can mushrooms

Salt and pepper

1 can cream of mushroom soup

1 cup sour cream

1/2 cup milk

2 tsp. Worcestershire sauce

Brown meat with salt, pepper, and garlic powder. Drain fat. Add onions and cook until onions begin to turn clear. Stir in remaining ingredients and cook over medium heat until bubbly. Serve over hot cooked egg noodles.

BAKED MAC AND CHEESE

2 cups macaroni

1/4 cup butter

3 Tbsp. flour

1 1/2 cups milk

1/2 onion, chopped

2 cups cheddar cheese, grated

4 slices sandwich bread

2 Tbsp. butter

1/4 cup Parmesan cheese

Cook and drain macaroni according to package directions. In a large heavy pot, melt butter. Add flour, and cook and stir until smooth. Slowly add milk, cooking and stirring until thickened. Remove from heat and stir in cheddar cheese and macaroni. Turn into greased 9x13 baking dish. Spread butter on both sides of bread. Grill on hot griddle or skillet. Cut grilled bread into small squares and toss over macaroni. Sprinkle with Parmesan cheese. Bake at 450 for 15-20 minutes.

PEPPER STEAK STIR~FRY

1 pound boneless beef sirloin steak, cut into thin strips
1 medium onion, thinly sliced
1 green bell pepper, thinly sliced
2 garlic cloves, minced
1/4 tsp. ground pepper

1 Tbsp. vegetable oil
1 cup water
1 tsp. beef bouillon
1 Tbsp. corn starch
Hot cooked rice

Heat oil in a large skillet. Cook steak, onions, peppers, and garlic in hot oil until onions begin to turn clear. Sprinkle with salt and pepper to taste. Dissolve bouillon in 1 cup water. Blend cornstarch with water. Add to steak and peppers and stir over medium heat until thickened and bubbly. Serve over Hot Cooked Rice.

PEPPER CHICKEN STIR~FRY

Follow recipe for Pepper Steak Stir-Fry, replacing the steak with 1 pound boneless, skinless chicken strips and replacing the beef bouillon with chicken bouillon.

VEGETABLE STIR~FRY

3-4 cups fresh vegetables of your choice:

onions, chopped

carrots, peeled and chopped

broccoli florets

zucchini, sliced

bell peppers, any color, chopped

bean sprouts

mushrooms

Stir-fry sauce:

1/2 tsp. garlic powder

2 Tbsp. soy sauce

2 Tbsp. hoisin sauce

1 Tbsp. honey

1 tsp. cornstarch

1/2 cup water

1 tsp. chicken bouillon

Heat 1 Tbsp. oil in large skillet. Stir-fry vegetables of choice until slightly tender but still crisp. Combine all ingredients for sauce, pour over vegetables, and stir over medium heat until thickened and vegetables are well coated. Serve over Hot Cooked Rice.

HOT COOKED RICE

Bring 4 cups water to boil in large pot. Stir in 2 Tbsp. butter, 1 tsp. salt, and 2 cups long-grain white rice. Cover with tight-fitting lid and reduce temperature to low. Simmer 20 minutes. Remove from heat and allow to sit 5 minutes. Makes 4 cups.

CHICKEN LO MEIN

1 pound boneless, skinless chicken strips
1/2 tsp. garlic powder
1/2 tsp. ground ginger
1 1/2 cups water
1 tsp. chicken bouillon
1 6-oz. pkg. lo mein noodles
1/2 onion, chopped

1 carrot, peeled and sliced
1 broccoli tree, chopped
2 cups cabbage, thinly sliced
2 stalks celery, thinly sliced
1 can bean sprouts, drained
1 tsp. cornstarch
2 Tbsp. soy sauce

Heat oil in a large skillet. Stir-fry chicken in hot oil over medium-high heat 4-5 minutes. Add garlic, ginger, water, and bouillon. Bring to a boil. Stir in vegetables and lo mein noodles. Cook 8-10 minutes or until vegetables are tender and noodles are done. Remove 1/2 cup of liquid and blend with cornstarch. Return to pan and stir over medium heat until liquid thickens. Stir in soy sauce and serve hot. Note: You can substitute 1 pound cooked and cubed ham for the chicken in this recipe.

VEGETABLE LO MEIN

Follow recipe for Chicken Lo Mein, replacing the chicken with sliced mushrooms, sliced water chestnuts, or both.

SESAME CHICKEN

1 pound boneless, skinless chicken strips
1/3 cup cornstarch
1/3 cup all-purpose flour

1 tsp. salt
3 eggs, well beaten
3 Tbsp. milk

Heat oil in heavy skillet. Blend cornstarch, flour, and salt together. Whisk eggs and milk together. Blend into dry mixture and stir well. Dip chicken in batter and drop into hot oil. Cook on both sides until golden brown. Drain on paper towel.

Sesame Sauce: Mix following with 2 cups water in medium saucepan--
1/2 cup brown sugar
1/2 cup white sugar
2 Tbsp. cornstarch

3 Tbsp. apple cider vinegar
3 Tbsp. soy sauce
1 Tbsp. sesame seeds

Cook and stir over medium-high heat until sauce thickens and boils. Pour sauce over cooked chicken strips. Serve with rice.

LEMON CHICKEN

Cook chicken as instructed in Sesame Chicken recipe. For lemon sauce, mix 1/2 cup white sugar, 2 Tbsp. cornstarch, 2 cups water, and 2 Tbsp. apple cider vinegar in a medium saucepan. Cook and stir over medium-high heat until thickened and boiling. Remove from heat. Stir in 1 tsp. lemon extract, 3 Tbsp. lemon juice, and 1 drop yellow food coloring. Pour over cooked chicken.

SWEET AND SOUR PORK

1 pound boneless pork, cut up
1/3 cup cornstarch
1/3 cup all-purpose flour
Vegetable oil, for cooking

1 tsp. salt
3 eggs, well beaten
3 Tbsp. milk

Heat oil in heavy skillet. Blend corn starch, flour, and salt together. Whisk eggs and milk together. Blend into dry mixture and stir well. Dip pork in batter and drop into hot oil. Cook on both sides until golden brown. Drain on paper towel.

Sweet and Sour Sauce:

1/2 cup brown sugar
1/2 tsp. chicken bouillon
1/4 cup cornstarch
2 cups water/pineapple juice
1 16-oz. can pineapple tidbits
3 Tbsp. apple cider vinegar

1/2 tsp. garlic powder
2 Tbsp. soy sauce
1 tsp. ground ginger
2 carrots, peeled and sliced
3 green onions, chopped
1 green bell pepper, chopped

Drain pineapple and reserve juice. Combine reserved pineapple juice and water to make 2 cups liquid. Mix liquid with remaining ingredients except cornstarch and pineapple in a large saucepan. Cook over medium heat until carrots are tender. Blend 1/2 cup water, 1 drop red food coloring, and cornstarch. Add to pan and stir over medium heat until sauce boils and thickens. Add pineapple and warm through. Pour over cooked pork pieces. Serve with rice.

SWEET AND SOUR CHICKEN

Follow the recipe for Sweet and Sour Pork, substituting boneless, skinless, chicken breast meat for the pork and omitting the red food coloring in the sauce. Pour over cooked chicken chunks. Serve with rice or chow mein noodles.

The Talmud

A child will tell in the street, what his father and mother say at home.

QUICK HAM FRIED RICE

2 cups cooked rice (day old)
2 Tbsp. vegetable oil
3 eggs, well beaten
1/2 cup ham, diced

2 green onions, chopped
1/2 cup frozen peas and carrots
1/2 tsp. chicken bouillon
2 tsp. soy sauce

Heat 1 Tbsp. oil in a large skillet. Scramble eggs. Remove eggs from skillet and heat remaining oil. Stir-fry ham and rice (day-old rice works best because it is drier than fresh-cooked rice) until ham starts to brown. Add green onions, peas, and carrots, and stir-fry until vegetables are cooked through. Sprinkle with bouillon and soy sauce. Return scrambled eggs to skillet and mix well.

SAUSAGE PRIMAVERA

12-oz. uncooked spaghetti

1 1/2 cups broccoli, chopped

1/2 green bell pepper, chopped

1/2 medium onion, chopped

3/4 pound smoked sausage, sliced

1/3 cup water

3/4 cup canned milk

2 Tbsp. butter

1/2 tsp. Italian seasoning

1/3 cup Parmesan cheese

Cook spaghetti, adding the vegetables during the last 4 minutes. Meanwhile, bring water and sausage to boil in a large skillet. Reduce heat. Cover and simmer 5 minutes. Add milk, butter, and Italian seasoning. Cook and stir until butter is melted. Drain spaghetti and vegetables and add to skillet. Remove skillet from heat and stir in the Parmesan cheese.

CABBAGE~BACON PASTA

1 12-oz. bag rainbow pasta, cooked
6 slices bacon, cooked and crumbled
1 head cabbage, sliced
2 carrots, peeled and shredded
1/2 onion, chopped
1/3 cup Parmesan cheese

In a large skillet cook bacon until well done. Crumble bacon but do not discard bacon drippings. Stir-fry vegetables in bacon drippings. Remove from heat. Fold in cooked pasta and Parmesan cheese.

BEEF AND BROCCOLI

1 pound boneless beef sirloin steak,
   cut into thin strips
1 medium onion, thinly sliced
3 cups chopped broccoli
2 garlic cloves, minced
1/4 tsp. ground pepper
1 Tbsp. vegetable oil
1 cup water
1 tsp. beef bouillon
1 Tbsp. cornstarch
2 Tbsp. soy sauce
Hot cooked rice

Steam broccoli until crisp-tender. Meanwhile, heat oil in a large skillet. Cook steak, onions, and garlic in hot oil until onions begin to turn clear. Sprinkle with pepper. Dissolve bouillon in 1 cup water. Blend cornstarch with water. Add to steak and stir over medium heat until thickened and bubbly. Add steamed broccoli and soy sauce and heat through. Serve over Hot Cooked Rice.

109

CHEESY BROCCOLI RICE

3 Tbsp. butter

1 cup vermicelli noodles, broken
   into 1-inch pieces

1 cup long grain white rice

2 tsp. chicken bouillon

3 cups water

2 cups chopped broccoli

1 cup milk

2 cups cheese, grated

Melt butter in large pot. Saute noodles and rice in butter until vermicelli starts to brown. Stir in bouillon and water. Place chopped broccoli on top of rice mixture, but don't stir. Reduce heat to low. Cover pot with tight fitting lid and simmer 20 minutes. Test rice; if water is gone and rice is not tender, add 1/2 cup water and continue cooking until rice is tender. Add milk and cheese and stir until cheese is melted. Serve hot.

A mother understands what her child does not say.

Jewish proverb

HAM AND BROCCOLI RICE

Follow recipe for Cheesy Broccoli Rice but saute 1/2 pound cooked and cubed ham along with the rice and vermicelli. Follow remainder of recipe.

EGG AND RICE WRAPS

3 Tbsp. butter

1 cup vermicelli noodles, broken
   into 1-inch pieces

1 cup long-grain white rice

2 tsp. chicken bouillon

3 cups water

6 eggs, well beaten

2 Tbsp. milk

6-8 flour tortillas

Mild salsa (opt.)

Melt butter in skillet that has a tight-fitting lid. Saute noodles and rice in butter until vermicelli starts to brown. Stir in bouillon and water. Reduce heat to low. Cover skillet with tight-fitting lid and simmer 20 minutes. Meanwhile, spray cooking spray in another skillet. Heat skillet. Pour beaten eggs and milk into hot skillet and cook and scramble eggs until done. Test rice; if water is gone and rice is not tender, add 1/2 cup water and continue cooking until rice is tender. Stir rice mixture into eggs. Warm tortillas and roll rice/egg mixture inside. Serve with salsa if desired.

BREAKFAST RICE WRAPS

Follow recipe for Egg and Rice Wraps, except add cooked sausage, bacon, or ham to rice/egg mixture for a quick and delicious breakfast wrap (this is a great way to use leftovers!). Serve with salsa if desired.

CREAMY MUSHROOM RICE

3 cups boiling water
1 1/2 cups long-grain rice
2 Tbsp. butter

1 can cream of mushroom soup
3/4 cup milk
1 cup fresh or frozen peas

Stir rice, 1 tsp. salt, and butter into boiling water. Cover and reduce heat to low. Simmer for 20 minutes. Remove from heat and stir in soup, milk, and peas.

COUNTRY~SEASONED RICE

2 Tbsp. butter
1 clove garlic, minced
1/4 cup onion, finely diced
2 green onions, chopped
1 cup long-grain rice

2 cups water
2 tsp. chicken bouillon
2 Tbsp. parsley flakes
1 tsp. Italian seasoning
1 bay leaf

Melt butter in medium saucepan. Saute onion and garlic until garlic is golden. Add rice and stir until coated with butter. Add water, bouillon, and herbs. Bring to a boil. Cover with tight-fitting lid. Reduce heat to low and simmer 20 minutes. Remove bay leaf. Serve with chicken or pork.

112

CHEESEBURGER RICE

1 1/2 pounds ground beef
3 cups cooked rice
1 30-oz. can stewed tomatoes

1 16-oz. can corn, drained
2 cups cheddar cheese, grated
Salt and pepper

Brown meat with salt, pepper, and garlic powder. Drain fat. Mix all ingredients together in a 9x13 dish. Bake at 350 for 30 minutes, until cheese is melted and bubbly.

 # SPANISH RICE

4 slices bacon
1/4 cup onions, diced
3 cups rice, cooked
1/4 cup salsa

1 30-oz. can crushed tomatoes
1 4-oz. can diced green chilis
1 16-oz. can corn, drained
1 cup cheddar cheese, grated

Cook bacon until crisp. Remove from pan and crumble. Saute onions in bacon fat until tender. Mix all ingredients except cheese in a 9x13 baking dish. Sprinkle cheese over top. Bake at 350 for 30 minutes or until cheese is melted and bubbly.

Elder Robert D. Hales said, "The key to strengthening our families is having the spirit of the Lord come into our homes."

I believe family mealtime is one way to bring that spirit into our homes . . . and soup seems to give us a head start on family mealtime. As soon as our children walk through the door and smell a pot of soup simmering, the aroma itself serves as a reminder that they are loved. They know they will be fed. They are secure that all is well. This security brings a peace and a comfort to their hearts even before the family gathers around the dinner table.

The following pages include some delicious soup recipes. I hope you will find a few that you will want to make again and again. Along with the soup recipes, I have included some bread recipes, because to me, soup and bread go hand-in hand. Have fun as you stir up these delicious soups and breads!

Wednesday

Soup and Bread

CHICKEN NOODLE SOUP

1 whole chicken (with skin and bone)
3 ribs celery (whole)
1 onion, quartered
2 tsp. salt
1 tsp. tarragon

6 carrots, peeled and sliced
1 onion, chopped
4 ribs celery, sliced
3 cups Egg Noodles
1 Tbsp. parsley flakes

Place 2 quarts water, chicken, and next four ingredients in a large soup pot. Simmer 1 hour or until chicken pulls away from bone. Strain broth and remove skin and bones from chicken. Discard skin, bones, celery, and onion. Return broth to pan. Add vegetables, parsley, salt, and pepper, and simmer 20 minutes. Remove chicken. Add homemade egg noodles and simmer 10 minutes. Meanwhile, cut cooked chicken into 1-inch chunks. Add chicken to pot. Bring to boil. Add egg noodles and cook 10-12 minutes or until noodles are done.

Egg Noodles:
Combine 3 well-beaten eggs, 1/3 cup milk, 1 tsp. oil, and 2 tsp. salt. Stir in flour (about 2 cups) until a stiff dough forms. Cover and let rest 10 minutes. Roll out to 1/16 inch thick. Roll up dough loosely. Cut into 1/4-inch wide strips. Unroll and cut strips into pieces 2 to 3 inches long. Use immediately or dry overnight before storing.

116

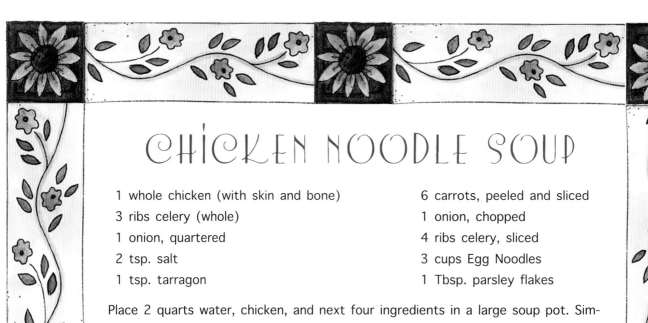

QUICK CHICKEN NOODLE SOUP

2 boneless, skinless chicken breast halves
1 cup water
2 tsp. chicken bouillon
1/4 tsp. paprika
4 carrots, peeled and sliced

3 ribs celery, sliced
1 onion, chopped
1 Tbsp. parsley flakes
2 cups water
3 cups egg noodles

Place chicken in water in soup pot. Sprinkle with bouillon and paprika. Add vegetables in order given. Sprinkle with parsley flakes. Cover and cook 30 minutes. Add 2 cups water. Bring soup to a full boil. Add egg noodles and cook 10-12 minutes or until noodles are done. Cut chicken into bite-sized chunks.

Each day of our lives, we make deposits in the memory banks of our children.

Charles R. Swindoll

CHICKEN AND RICE SOUP

Follow recipe for Quick Chicken Noodle Soup, replacing the egg noodles with 1 1/2 cups long-grain white rice. Cover and cook 25 minutes or until rice is tender.

CHICKEN DUMPLING SOUP

Follow the recipe for Chicken Noodle Soup, replacing the egg noodles with Dumpling Biscuit Mix (below).

If you want to make quick chicken and dumplings, follow the Quick Chicken Noodle Soup recipe and use 2 packages refrigerator biscuits in place of the Dumpling Biscuit Mix.

Dumpling Biscuit Mix:
1 1/2 cups all-purpose flour
1 Tbsp. baking powder
1/4 tsp. baking soda
2 Tbsp. sugar
1/2 tsp. salt
1/2 cup butter
1/3 cup milk

Sift dry ingredients in large bowl. Cut in butter until mixture is coarse and crumbly. Add milk and mix together quickly just until dough is formed. Drop large spoonfuls of dough into boiling soup. Cook 15 minutes or until done in center.

118

CHICKEN VEGETABLE STEW

2 14 1/2-oz. cans chicken broth
2 cups water
1 cup frozen mixed vegetables
1 1/2 cups chicken, cooked and cubed

1/4 tsp. thyme
1/4 tsp. salt
2 Tbsp. parsley flakes
1 cup small shell pasta

In large saucepan, bring broth and water to a boil. Add vegetables and return to a boil. Add pasta, chicken, thyme, and parsley flakes. Boil 7-9 minutes or until pasta and vegetables are tender. Sprinkle with salt and pepper.

SOUTHWEST TURKEY SOUP

3 cups turkey, cooked and cubed
1 can black beans, drained and rinsed
1 16-oz. can diced tomatoes
1 4-oz. can diced green chiles
1 16-oz. can corn, drained, or
1 1/2 cups frozen corn

2 Tbsp. butter
1 med. onion, chopped
2 cups water
1 cube chicken bouillon
1 1/2 tsp. chili powder
1/4 tsp. cayenne or red pepper

Melt butter in large soup pot. Saute onion in butter until tender. Stir remainder of ingredients in a pot and simmer on medium-low heat 30 minutes or until heated through. Serve hot with corn chips and sour cream.

VEGETABLE BEEF SOUP

1/4 cup all-purpose flour
1 1/2 pounds beef stew meat
1 Tbsp. vegetable oil
1 tsp. garlic powder
3 tsp. beef bouillon
1 medium onion, chopped
3 potatoes, peeled and cubed

3 carrots, peeled and sliced
2 celery ribs, sliced
2 quarts water
1 16-oz. can whole-kernel corn
1 16-oz. can green beans
1 16-oz. can stewed tomatoes
1 cup frozen peas

Put flour in large bag. Cut stew meat into 1-inch cubes. Shake meat pieces in bag to coat. Heat oil in large soup pot. Brown stew meat a few pieces at a time. Add garlic powder, bouillon, onion, potatoes, carrots, celery, and water. Bring to a boil. Reduce heat, cover, and simmer 30-45 minutes or until meat is tender. Stir in the rest of vegetables and season with salt and pepper. Simmer 10 minutes.

VEGETABLE BEEF STEW

Follow recipe for Vegetable Beef Soup, but reduce water to 1 quart and omit the canned vegetables.

HAMBURGER SOUP

1 1/2 pounds hamburger
1 tsp. celery salt
2 tsp. beef bouillon
1/2 onion, chopped
3 carrots, peeled and sliced

3 potatoes, peeled and chopped
2 celery ribs, sliced
2 quarts water
1 16-oz. can whole-kernel corn
Salt and pepper

Brown hamburger in large soup pot. Drain fat. Add remaining ingredients. Bring to a boil. Reduce heat and simmer 30-40 minutes or until carrots are tender.

QUICK TOMATO SOUP

3 Tbsp. butter
3 Tbsp. flour
2 8-oz. cans tomato sauce
4 cups water

Melt butter in medium saucepan. Stir in flour and cook until bubbly. Slowly pour in water while continually stirring. Add tomato sauce and continue cooking and stirring until soup comes to a boil. Season with salt and pepper if desired.

121

MEATBALL SPAGHETTI SOUP

1 pound ground beef
1/2 tsp. salt
1/4 tsp. pepper
1/2 tsp. garlic powder

4 cups water
1 1/2 cups spaghetti noodles
2 quarts spaghetti sauce
1 tsp. salt

Mix ground beef with seasonings. Shape into 2-inch balls and brown in skillet for 15-20 minutes. Place on paper towel to drain fat. Meanwhile, break spaghetti into 3- to 4-inch pieces. Bring water and 1 tsp. salt to boil in a large pot. Add noodles and about 10 minutes or until spaghetti is tender. Do not drain. Stir in meatballs and spaghetti sauce. Cook until thoroughly heated. If desired, sprinkle individual servings with grated Parmesan cheese.

CHEESY RAVIOLI SOUP

1 12-oz. pkg. cheese ravioli
4 cups water

1 tsp. salt
2 quarts spaghetti sauce

Bring water to boil in large soup pot. Add ravioli and cook 10 minutes. Do not drain. Add 2 quarts spaghetti sauce and cook until thoroughly heated. If desired, sprinkle individual servings with grated Parmesan cheese.

122

LORI'S TORTILLA STEW

2 chicken breasts (with bone and skin)
2 cups water
1 tsp. chicken bouillon
1/2 tsp. paprika
1 16-oz. can Mexican stewed tomatoes
1 4-oz. can diced green chiles

1/2 onion, diced
1 tsp. chili powder
1/2 tsp. garlic powder
tortilla chips
Monterrey Jack cheese
sour cream

Place chicken, water, and bouillon in medium saucepan. Sprinkle paprika over chicken. Cover and let simmer 30 minutes or until chicken falls away from the bone. Skin and bone chicken. Discard bones and skin. Cut chicken and return to pan. Add next six ingredients and simmer 30 minutes. Serve with chips, grated Monterrey Jack cheese, sour cream, and avocados (optional).

EASY TACO SOUP

1 pound hamburger
3 Tbsp. taco seasoning
1 can chili con carne
1 can whole-kernel corn

1/2 cup mild salsa
1 cup water
Corn tortilla chips
Choice of toppings

Brown hamburger and drain fat. Mix meat with next five ingredients. Simmer 20-30 minutes. Serve over chips and top with sour cream, grated cheese, and other toppings of choice (lettuce, tomatoes, olives, peppers, etc.).

123

CREAMED ZUCCHINI SOUP

2 tsp. cooking oil
1 medium onion, chopped
1 clove garlic, minced
4 medium zucchini, chopped
2 tsp. chicken bouillon

1 Tbsp. lemon juice
3 cups water
1/2 cup grated cheese
1/2 cup sour cream

In large saucepan heat oil over medium-low heat. Saute onion and garlic about 5 minutes or until soft. Stir in zucchini, chicken bouillon, lemon juice, and water. Bring to a boil. Reduce heat and simmer 15 minutes. Puree mixture in food processor or blender. Pour into serving dish and quickly whisk in cheese and sour cream.

BROCCOLI CHEESE SOUP

1 small onion, chopped
2 Tbsp. butter
3 Tbsp. flour
2 cups milk
1 cup broccoli, chopped and cooked

2 tsp. chicken bouillon
Salt and pepper
1/2 tsp. thyme
1 Tbsp. garlic salt
2 cups cheese, grated

Saute onion in butter until tender. Stir in flour until smooth. Gradually add milk, 1 cup water, and bouillon. Cook and stir until thickened. Add salt and pepper, thyme, garlic salt, and cheese. Heat through. Stir in cooked broccoli and serve.

CREAM OF BROCCOLI SOUP

2 cups water
4 potatoes, peeled and chopped
2 stalks broccoli, chopped
1 carrot, peeled and grated

1 tsp. chicken bouillon
1 can cream of chicken soup
1 cup sour cream

In saucepan, dissolve bouillon in water. Layer potatoes, broccoli, and carrots in that order in pan, sprinkling a little salt over each layer. Cover and simmer 20 minutes or until broccoli is tender but not mushy. Turn off heat. Mash vegetables lightly with potato masher. Stir in soup and sour cream.

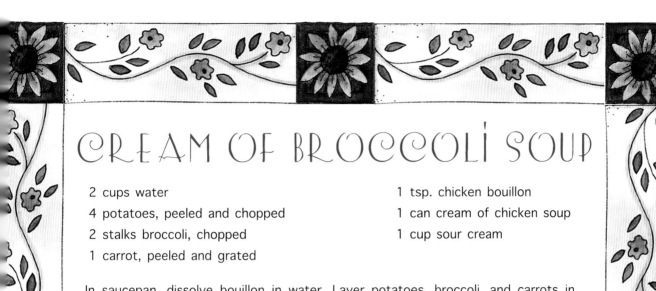

POTATO CHOWDER

8 slices bacon, cut into 1-inch pieces
6 new red potatoes, chopped
1 cup onion, chopped
1 can cream of chicken soup
1/4 tsp. ground black pepper

1 1/4 cups milk
1 can whole-kernel corn, drained
1 cup sour cream
1/4 tsp. thyme leaves

Cook bacon 2-3 minutes in large soup pot. Drain fat. Add potatoes and onion. Continue cooking over medium heat for 15-20 minutes or until potatoes are tender and bacon is just crisp, stirring occasionally. Stir in remaining ingredients and heat through.

125

CREAMED CORN CHOWDER

1 8-oz. pkg. cream cheese

2 cups sour cream

Juice of 1 lemon

Salt and pepper to taste

1/4 tsp. garlic powder

4 Tbsp. butter

4 Tbsp. flour

3 cups milk

1 can creamed corn

1-2 cups croutons

Beat cream cheese until smooth. Add sour cream, lemon juice, and seasonings and mix well. Melt butter in soup pot. Add flour and stir until bubbly. Slowly add milk, stirring constantly to make a smooth white sauce. Add corn and cream cheese mixture and heat through, stirring until well blended. Serve with croutons.

Nothing says HOME like a warm bowl of soup!

CARROT CHOWDER

2 cups water

1 tsp. chicken bouillon

3 carrots, peeled and shredded

3 medium potatoes chopped

1 medium onion, chopped

1/4 tsp. ground ginger

1 cup sour cream

1/2 cup milk

Dissolve bouillon in water in a soup pot. Place next four ingredients in pot in order. Simmer on medium-low heat until potatoes are tender (about 30 minutes). Mash lightly and stir in sour cream and milk.

COUNTRY CABBAGE SOUP

1/2 pound ground beef
4 cups green cabbage, shredded
1 cup potatoes, finely diced
1 cup carrots, finely diced
1/2 cup onion, finely diced

3 Tbsp. butter
1 Tbsp. flour
1 1/2 cups beef broth
1 can evaporated milk
Salt and pepper

Brown beef in large saucepan and drain excess fat. Add cabbage, potatoes, carrots, and onion. Stir in butter and cook until potatoes are tender but not brown, about 5 minutes. Stir in flour. Add remaining ingredients and simmer about 20 minutes.

CREAMY VEGETABLE SOUP

4 potatoes, peeled and chopped
2 Tbsp. butter
3 medium carrots, thinly sliced
1 medium pepper, chopped
1 medium onion, chopped

1 16-oz. can stewed tomatoes
1 tsp. chicken bouillon
2 cups water
1 can evaporated milk

Combine bouillon, water, and potatoes in large soup pot and cook until potatoes are tender. Blend in food processor or blender until smooth. Melt butter in skillet. Saute very thin carrots, peppers, and onions until lightly browned and softened. Drain juice from tomatoes and add stewed tomatoes to vegetables. Continue cooking over medium heat. Return potatoes to soup pot. Stir in vegetables and milk. Heat through.

127

SPLIT PEA SOUP

1 pound dry green split peas

1 ham hock

1 cup onion, chopped

2 tsp. chicken bouillon

2 quarts water

Salt and pepper

1 cup carrots, diced

1 cup celery, diced

1/2 cup light cream

2 Tbsp. butter

Combine peas, ham hock, onion, bouillon, water, salt, and pepper in a large soup pot. Bring to a boil. Cover and simmer 2 hours, stirring frequently. Remove ham bone, debone, and return meat to soup. Meanwhile, simmer carrots and celery until tender. Stir cream and butter into soup and heat through.

CHEDDAR CHOWDER

2 cups water

2 cups potatoes, diced

1/2 cup carrots, diced

1/2 cup celery, diced

1/4 cup onion, chopped

Salt and pepper

3 Tbsp. butter

1/4 cup flour

1 can evaporated milk

2 cups cheddar cheese, grated

Combine water, potatoes, carrots, celery, onion, salt, and pepper in large soup pot and cook 10-12 minutes. Meanwhile, melt butter in small saucepan. Stir in flour until smooth and bubbly. Slowly add milk and cook until thickened. Stir in cheese until melted. Drain vegetables thoroughly and stir into cheese sauce. Heat through.

CLAM CHOWDER

4 slices bacon, cut up

2 6 1/2-oz. cans minced clams

5 potatoes, peeled and diced

1/2 cup onions, chopped

1/2 cup celery, finely diced

3 Tbsp. flour

1 cup milk

1 can evaporated milk

1 tsp. Worcestershire sauce

Cook bacon in soup pot until crisp. Do not drain bacon fat. Drain clams, reserving liquid. Add enough water to make 2 cups liquid. Add liquid and vegetables to the cooked bacon. Cover and simmer 20 minutes or until potatoes are tender. Blend flour and the 1 cup milk together, stirring the milk in slowly to prevent lumps. Add flour mixture and clams to soup. Cook and stir over medium heat until thickened and bubbly. Add canned milk and Worcestershire sauce. Sprinkle with salt and pepper.

A Mother's Love

While the soup or sauce is simmering, take a moment to place your child on your lap. Whisper a story in his ear or sing a favorite song to him. For years to come; whenever he smells the familiar aroma of what you were cooking, this sweet memory will flood back into his mind, and he will again feel comfort; remembering his sweet mother's love.

129

PARMESAN HERB LOAF

1 pkg. active dry yeast
1/2 cup warm water
3 cups flour
1/2 cup parmesan cheese
1 Tbsp. sugar
1 Tbsp. minced onion

1 Tbsp. Italian seasoning
1 tsp. baking soda
1/2 tsp. salt
1 cup sour cream
1/3 cup milk

Dissolve yeast in warm water. Add remaining ingredients and mix well. Knead 5-6 minutes or until dough is smooth and elastic. Place in greased bowl in a warm area and allow to raise 30 minutes. Shape in loaf and place in greased loaf pan. Let raise until double. Bake at 350 for 30-40 minutes or until bread makes a hollow sound when you thump the center of loaf. Remove from pan and allow to cool on wire rack.

CHEESE TOPPED HERB LOAF

Follow recipe for Parmesan Herb Loaf but sprinkle 1/2 cup grated cheddar cheese on top of loaf after loaf has baked 15 minutes. Return to oven for 15-20 minutes until cheese bubbles and browns and becomes crispy. Cool on wire rack.

130

MEXICAN CORN BREAD

2 cups all-purpose flour

1 cup cornmeal

2 Tbsp. baking powder

1 tsp. salt

1 4-oz. can diced green chilies

1/2 cup frozen or canned corn

2 eggs

1/2 cup sour cream

1/2 cup vegetable oil

1/2 cup milk

Grease an 8-inch square pan and line the bottom with waxed paper. In a large bowl, sift dry ingredients together. Beat the eggs together with the sour cream, oil, and milk. Pour mixture into dry ingredients. Add the green chilies and corn and mix well. Pour into prepared pan. Bake in preheated oven at 400 for 20-25 minutes, or until loaf has risen and is lightly browned.

CHEESY CORN BREAD

Follow recipe for Mexican Corn Bread, but add 1 cup grated cheddar cheese in place of the diced green chilies. Bake as directed.

Note: You can leave the green chilies in this recipe for another variation.

131

CHEESY POTATO BREAD

2 cups all-purpose flour

1 tsp. salt

1/2 tsp. dry mustard

2 tsp. baking powder

1/2 cup cheddar cheese, grated

3/4 cup mashed potatoes

3/4 cup water

2 Tbsp. oil

Sift first four ingredients. Reserve 1/4 cup cheese. Stir remaining cheese and potatoes into flour mixture. Add water and oil. Mix to make a soft dough. Turn onto floured surface and shape into 8-inch circle. Place on greased pizza pan. Sprinkle with the reserved cheese. Bake at 425 for 25-30 minutes. Cool on wire rack.

ENGLISH MUFFIN BREAD

1 pkg. dry yeast

3 cups flour

2 tsp. sugar

1 tsp. salt

1/4 tsp. baking soda

1 cup milk

1/4 cup water

Yellow cornmeal

Combine yeast, 1 1/2 cups flour, sugar, salt, and baking soda. Heat milk and water until very warm. Add to dry mixture and beat well. Add remaining 1 1/2 cups flour to make a stiff batter. Grease two loaf pans and dust with cornmeal. Pour batter into loaf pans and sprinkle with cornmeal. Cover and let raise 45 minutes. Bake at 400 for 25-30 minutes. Cool on wire rack. Before serving, slice and toast.

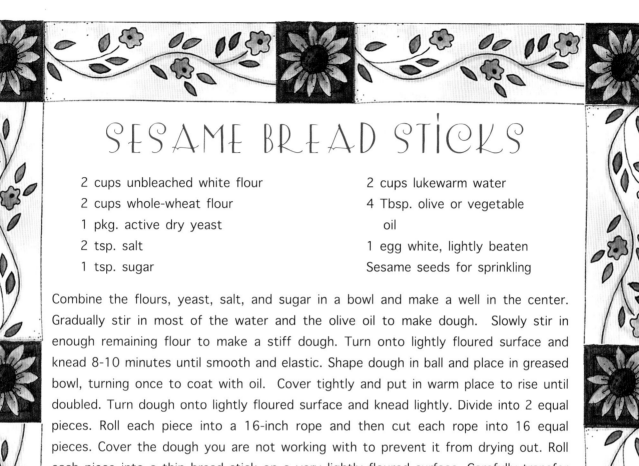

SESAME BREAD STICKS

2 cups unbleached white flour
2 cups whole-wheat flour
1 pkg. active dry yeast
2 tsp. salt
1 tsp. sugar

2 cups lukewarm water
4 Tbsp. olive or vegetable
   oil
1 egg white, lightly beaten
Sesame seeds for sprinkling

Combine the flours, yeast, salt, and sugar in a bowl and make a well in the center. Gradually stir in most of the water and the olive oil to make dough. Slowly stir in enough remaining flour to make a stiff dough. Turn onto lightly floured surface and knead 8-10 minutes until smooth and elastic. Shape dough in ball and place in greased bowl, turning once to coat with oil. Cover tightly and put in warm place to rise until doubled. Turn dough onto lightly floured surface and knead lightly. Divide into 2 equal pieces. Roll each piece into a 16-inch rope and then cut each rope into 16 equal pieces. Cover the dough you are not working with to prevent it from drying out. Roll each piece into a thin bread stick on a very lightly floured surface. Carefully transfer to greased baking sheet. Cover and set aside to raise for 10 minutes. Brush with egg white. Sprinkle evenly and thickly with sesame seeds. Bake at 450 for 10 minutes. Brush again with egg white and bake an additional 5 minutes or until golden brown and crisp. Cool on wire rack.

Children need LOVE...
               especially when they least deserve it.

133

DILLY CASSEROLE BREAD

1 Tbsp. active dry yeast

1/3 cup warm water

2 Tbsp. sugar

1 cup cottage cheese

1/4 cup butter

2 Tbsp. dried minced onions

2 tsp. dill seed

1 tsp. salt

1/4 tsp. baking soda

1 egg

2 1/2 cups flour

Dissolve yeast in warm water. Add sugar. Heat cottage cheese to lukewarm. Blend cottage cheese, dissolved yeast, and remaining ingredients in large mixing bowl. Stir well. Place in a warm area to raise until doubled (about 1 hour). Stir down and pour into a greased 2 1/2-quart casserole dish. Let raise 30 minutes. Bake at 350 for 40-50 minutes.

May Love be the Heart of this home.

134

FRESH HOAGIE BUNS

2 pkgs. active dry yeast
1 1/2 cups warm water
1 Tbsp. sugar

2 Tbsp. butter, softened
4-5 cups bread flour
2 tsp. salt

Dissolve yeast in warm water. Stir in sugar and butter. Sift 3 cups flour with salt in large mixing bowl. Pour yeast mixture in and beat until smooth. Continue adding flour until a stiff dough forms. Turn onto floured surface and knead 10-12 minutes. Cover and let rest 20 minutes. Shape dough into 6 large hoagie buns. Place on greased baking sheet. Brush with vegetable oil. Cover with plastic wrap and refrigerate at least 2 hours. Remove from refrigerator and let stand 10 minutes. Slit tops of buns. Bake at 425 for 15 minutes.

PITA POCKET BREAD

1 tsp. active dry yeast
1/2 c. warm water

1 1/4 c. flour
1/2 tsp. salt

Dissolve yeast in warm water. Add flour and salt, and stir to make a soft dough. Knead well, adding a little flour if needed. Place in greased bowl. Cover and let rise 15 minutes. Divide dough into 4 balls. Cover and let rise 10 minutes. Flatten each ball and use rolling pin to roll into a thin circle (about 1/4 inch thick). Place on greased baking sheet. Bake at 500 for 4-6 minutes until puffed and lightly browned.

135

BUTTERMILK BISCUITS

1 1/2 cups all-purpose flour
1 Tbsp. baking powder
1/4 tsp. baking soda
2 Tbsp. sugar
1/2 tsp. salt

1/2 cup butter or shortening
1/3 cup buttermilk
2 Tbsp. heavy cream or
   melted butter

Sift dry ingredients together in large bowl. Cut in butter or shortening until mixture is coarse and crumbly. Cover and refrigerate 20 minutes or more. Make a well in center of mixture and add enough buttermilk to hold dough together. Mix quickly with your fingers just until dough forms. Turn onto lightly floured surface and roll to 3/4 inch thick. Cut with biscuit cutter and place on ungreased baking sheet. Brush tops with cream or melted butter. Bake at 400 for 13-15 minutes or until lightly golden. Cool on wire rack.

CHEESE~TOPPED BISCUITS

Follow recipe for Buttermilk Biscuits. Grate 1/2 cup cheddar cheese and sprinkle over biscuits before baking. Follow baking directions and cool on wire rack.

SOURDOUGH STARTER

1 Tbsp. active dry yeast
2 cups warm water

2 cups unbleached flour
1/4 cup sugar

Dissolve yeast in warm water in a 2-quart canning jar or plastic container. Do not use metal. Let stand for 10 minutes. Stir in flour and sugar. Cover and let stand at room temperature until bubbly and sour (about 2 days). Use a portion for a recipe and add to your starter: 1 cup flour, 1 cup milk, and 1/4 cup sugar. Store at room temperature, stirring it down every day and taking some from it each week for recipes.

SOURDOUGH BISCUITS

1 cup sourdough starter
1 cup warm water
1/2 tsp. baking soda
1/2 cup vegetable oil

1 egg, well beaten
1 tsp. salt
1/4 cup sugar
4 1/2 to 5 cups all-purpose flour

Combine first five ingredients in glass or plastic bowl. Add salt, sugar, and 2 cups of the flour. Stir until smooth. Continue adding flour and stirring until sides of bowl are clean. Turn onto floured surface and knead 6-8 minutes. Shape into 24 biscuits and place on greased baking sheet. Cover and let raise in warm place until double (about 1 hour). Bake at 350 for 15-20 minutes.

BASIC WHITE BREAD

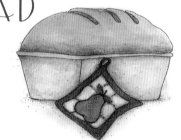

1 Tbsp. active dry yeast
1 1/2 cups water
3 Tbsp. sugar
1/4 cup butter

5 cups bread flour
1 1/2 tsp. salt
3 Tbsp. powdered milk

Dissolve yeast in warm water. Add sugar, butter, 2 cups flour, salt, and powdered milk. Beat at low speed with electric mixer 1 minute, and then on high for 2 minutes. Stir in as much remaining flour as you can stir in by hand. Turn onto floured surface and knead 8-10 minutes, adding enough flour to make a moderately stiff dough. Place in greased bowl and cover. Let raise until double. Punch down dough. Divide dough and shape into two loaves. Place in greased loaf pans and cover. Let raise until double. Bake at 375 for 35-45 minutes or until crust is golden brown. Cool on rack for 10 minutes. Remove from loaf pans and cool on rack.

WHOLE~WHEAT BREAD

Follow recipe for Basic White Bread, but substitute 3 tablespoons honey for the sugar, 2 tablespoons vegetable oil for the butter, and whole-wheat flour for the bread flour. Add 1-2 tsp. vital wheat gluten (optional) for a lighter bread. Continue as directed.

138

SOFT PRETZELS

1 pkg. active dry yeast

1 1/2 cups warm water

1/4 cup brown sugar

4 1/2 cups flour

Baking soda

Kosher salt

Combine yeast, warm water, and sugar together. Let stand 5 minutes. Add flour and beat with dough hook or knead on floured surface 6-7 minutes or until smooth. Let rest 5-10 minutes. Meanwhile, fill a saucepan 3/4 full with water. For every cup of water, add 2 teaspoons baking soda to the pan. Bring water and soda to a boil. Divide dough into 12 pieces. Roll each piece into a rope and fold into a pretzel. Drop each pretzel in boiling water for about 10 seconds. Remove with a slotted spoon. Place pretzels on greased baking sheet and sprinkle with kosher salt. Bake at 450 for 8-9 minutes or until golden brown.

HEARTY BAGELS

Follow recipe for Soft Pretzels, but if desired, add ingredients such as nuts or fruits when mixing in the flour. Knead in additional flour to make a stiff dough. Let rest 10 minutes. Divide dough into 12 pieces. Shape each piece into a flattened round disk. Press thumbs into center and pull dough outward to make a center hole. Continue cooking and baking as directed.

PARKER HOUSE ROLLS

1 pkg. active dry yeast
1/2 cup warm water
1/3 cup sugar
1 tsp. baking powder
1/2 cup butter

1 cup milk
1 tsp. salt
2 eggs, beaten
4 1/2 cups flour

Dissolve yeast in warm water. Add sugar and baking powder and let rest. Melt butter. Add milk and salt. Cool slightly. Stir into yeast mixture. Add eggs. Gradually add flour until well mixed. Cover and refrigerate. About 2 hours before serving, roll out dough to 1/2 inch thick. Cut with biscuit cutter, score with a knife across middle, and fold over. Place in greased baking pan with rolls touching. Bake at 425 for 12-14 minutes or until golden brown. Brush with butter.

MARIANNE DINNER ROLLS

Follow Parker House Rolls recipe for dough. To prepare rolls, grease two 12-cup muffin tins. Roll dough to 1/8 inch thick. Cut 2x7-inch strips. Roll up cinnamon roll-style and place in muffin cups. Let raise 30 minutes. Bake at 400 for 12-15 minutes or until golden brown. Remove from oven and glaze.
Glaze:
Mix 2 Tbsp. orange juice with 1 cup powdered sugar and beat until creamy. Glaze rolls while still hot. Remove from muffin tins after glaze cools.

ANGEL YEAST BISCUITS

1 pkg. active dry yeast
1/2 cup warm water
5 cups flour
1/4 cup sugar
1 tsp. baking soda
3 tsp. baking powder
1 tsp. salt
3/4 cup butter
2 cups buttermilk

Dissolve yeast in warm milk. Sift dry ingredients together. Cut in butter until crumbly. Add buttermilk and yeast and stir until well blended. Place dough in a greased bowl. Cover and refrigerate until ready to use. Roll dough to 1/2 inch thick on a lightly floured surface. Cut with biscuit cutter. Placed on greased baking sheet and let raise until doubled, 30-45 minutes. Bake at 400 for 10-15 minutes.

"Give us this day our daily bread"

Matthew 6:11

I think the most important reason we should gather together as a family around the dinner table is that it gives us the opportunity to express gratitude. One of the great tragedies of our day is that millions of people receive their dinner through a drive-up window and gobble it down without a thought as to who provided that food for them. We have a sacred duty to teach our children to thank God daily for the great prosperity we enjoy.

141

If someone were to ask me to name a dish that represents "family," I would have to say "casseroles." The individuals in a family are like the ingredients that we use in a casserole. Each person is unique and important, just as each casserole ingredient has its own unique texture and flavor. But even though each one is unique and different, they are equally important. A carrot may not taste like an onion, but does that make the carrot less important than the onion? Although an onion boasts its own unique and individual flavor, it is most delicious when combined with other flavors. It's the same with us: even though individuals are each important in their own way, they are even more important in the family. If every member of the family does his or her personal part, they blend together, and the result is something that is much better than each individual alone. We are happiest when we recognize how much we need each other.

That was a long description for casseroles. So let me just say that whether it's family or food, I love it when they all come together!

I hope you enjoy blending both these recipes and your family!

Thursday
Casseroles

TEXAS CORN BREAD

1 pound ground beef
1 small onion, chopped
2 jalapeno peppers, seeded and diced
1 cup flour
1 cup corn meal
1 Tbsp. baking powder
1/2 tsp. baking soda

1 tsp. salt
1 can cream-style corn
1 cup milk
1/2 cup vegetable oil
2 eggs, well beaten
3 cups cheddar cheese, grated

Brown meat with salt, pepper, and garlic powder. Drain fat. Combine meat with onions and peppers, and spread in a 9x13 casserole dish. Combine remaining ingredients until well blended. Spread over meat mixture. Bake at 425 for 20 minutes or until crust is golden brown. Cut and serve.

CHILI CASSEROLE

2 cups elbow macaroni
1 15-oz. can chili con carne
1 16-oz. can whole-kernel corn

1 cup sour cream
1 cup cheddar cheese, grated

Cook macaroni according to package directions. Drain and return to pot. Add remaining ingredients and mix well. Serve right out of the pot.

144

ONION RING CASSEROLE

1/2 pound ground beef

1 16-oz. pkg. frozen peas

1 can cream of mushroom soup

2 cups frozen hash browns

1/2 tsp. salt

20 frozen onion rings

1 cup cheddar cheese, grated

Brown meat with salt, pepper, and garlic powder. Drain fat. Spread meat in 9x13 casserole dish. Layer remaining ingredients, except cheese, in order given. Bake at 400 for 30 minutes. Sprinkle cheese on top and bake 10 minutes more.

When you teach your son, you teach your son's son.

The Talmud

BEEFARONI BAKE

1 pound ground beef

2 cups cheddar cheese, shredded

2 cans tomato sauce

2 Tbsp. butter

1 16-oz. pkg. elbow
macaroni

Brown meat with salt, pepper, and garlic powder. Drain fat. Cook macaroni according to package directions. Combine all ingredients, reserving 1 cup cheese, in a 9x13 casserole dish. Sprinkle remaining cheese on top. Bake at 350 for 30 minutes or until cheese is melted and bubbly.

145

BEEF AND SPINACH BAKE

1 pound ground beef
1 medium onion, chopped
1 garlic clove, minced
1 4-oz. can mushrooms
Salt and pepper

1 tsp. dried oregano
2 10-oz. pkgs. frozen spinach
1 can cream of mushroom soup
1 cup sour cream
2 cups mozzarella cheese, shredded

Cook beef, onion, and garlic over medium heat. Drain fat. Stir in mushrooms, salt, pepper, and oregano. Spread in a 9x13 casserole dish. Place spinach over meat mixture. Mix soup, sour cream, and 1 cup cheese together. Spread over spinach. Bake at 350 for 20 minutes. Sprinkle with remaining cheese, and bake additional 10 minutes.

HAMBURGER CASSEROLE

1 1/2 pounds ground beef
1 16-oz. pkg. frozen peas
1 can cream of mushroom soup

1/2 cup milk
3 cups hash browns
1/2 tsp. paprika

Brown meat with salt, pepper, and garlic powder. Drain fat. Spread meat in 9x13 baking pan. Layer remaining ingredients in order given. Bake at 400 for 30 minutes.

146

GREEN BEAN CASSEROLE

2 Tbsp. butter
1 small onion, diced
2 cans French-sliced green beans
1 can cream of mushroom soup

Salt and pepper
1 cup milk
1 box chicken stuffing
Bacon bits (opt.)

Saute onion in butter until onion starts to brown. Drain green beans and spread in a 9x13 casserole dish. Cover with cream of mushroom soup. Pour milk over soup and sprinkle with sauteed onions, stuffing mix, and bacon bits if desired. Bake at 350 for 30 minutes. Serve warm.

ZUCCHINI CASSEROLE

4 cups zucchini, chopped
1 cup onion, chopped
1 cup carrots, grated
1 can cream of chicken soup

1 cup cheddar cheese, grated
1 cup sour cream
1 box chicken stuffing mix

Steam zucchini, onions, and carrots 10 minutes or until zucchini is tender but still firm. In a 9x13 casserole dish, combine soup, cheese, and sour cream. Drain vegetables. Use water from vegetables to make stuffing. Prepare stuffing according to package directions. Stir vegetables into soup mixture. Sprinkle stuffing over top. Bake at 350 for 30 minutes.

147

ENCHILADA CASSEROLE

1 1/2 pounds ground beef
2 cups cheese, shredded
1 can cream of mushroom soup
1 cup sour cream
1/2 cup milk
1 16-oz. can enchilada sauce
1 4-oz. can diced green chilies
10 corn tortillas

Brown meat with salt, pepper, and garlic powder. Drain fat. Mix meat with remaining ingredients except 1 cup shredded cheese and tortillas. Spread mixture in 9x13 dish. Tear tortillas and fold into mixture. Sprinkle with remaining cheese. Bake at 350 for 30 minutes or until cheese is melted and bubbly. Serve with sour cream, salsa, and choice of toppings.

BURRITO CASSEROLE

10 flour tortillas
1 can refried beans
2 cups cheddar cheese, shredded
1 4-oz. can green chilies
1 can cream of chicken soup
1/2 cup milk
1 16-oz. can enchilada sauce
1 cup ripe olives

Fill tortillas with beans and cheese. Fold in sides and roll up for burritos. Place burritos in greased 9x13 baking pan. Combine remaining ingredients, reserving 1/2 cup shredded cheese, and pour over burritos. Sprinkle with cheese. Bake at 350 for 30 minutes or until cheese is melted and bubbly.

CORN CHIPS CASSEROLE

1 1/2 pounds ground beef
2 cups cheddar cheese, shredded
1 16-oz. can corn, drained
1 15-oz. can chili con carne

1/2 cup mild salsa
4 cups corn tortilla chips
1 cup ripe olives, sliced
1 cup sour cream

Brown meat with salt, pepper, and garlic powder. Drain fat. Combine all ingredients except the olives and sour cream. Turn into a 9x13 casserole dish. Bake at 350 for 30 minutes. Remove from oven. Drop dollops of sour cream over top of casserole and sprinkle with sliced olives.

CHICKEN ENCHILADA CASSEROLE

1 cup chicken, cooked and shredded
2 4-oz. cans diced green chilies
1 cup Monterrey Jack cheese, grated

1 can cream of chicken soup
1 cup sour cream
10 yellow corn tortillas

Mix all ingredients except tortillas in 9x13 casserole dish. Tear tortillas into 2" pieces. Fold tortillas into the mixture. Bake at 350 for 30 minutes. Serve with lettuce, sour cream, fresh-cut tomatoes, and salsa; top with an olive.

CHEESY BROCCOLI

3 Tbsp. butter
1 pound ham, cooked and cubed
2 cups cooked rice
2 cups broccoli, chopped
1 med. onion, chopped

1 celery rib, chopped
1/2 tsp. poultry seasoning
1 can cream of celery soup
2 cups cheddar cheese, grated

Saute onion and celery in butter. Add broccoli and 1/2 cup water. Cover and simmer 5-6 minutes until broccoli is crisp-tender. Combine all ingredients in a greased 9x13 casserole dish, reserving 1 cup cheese. Sprinkle with remaining cheese. Bake at 350 for 30 minutes or until cheese is melted and bubbly.

CREAMED HAM BAKE

3 cups egg noodles, cooked
1 pound ham, cooked and cubed
1 8-oz. pkg. cream cheese
1 cup sour cream

1/2 cup milk
1/4 cup Parmesan cheese
1 cup mozzarella cheese, grated
1/2 cup green onions, chopped

Spread cooked egg noodles in greased 9x13 baking pan. Combine remaining ingredients. Pour over noodles. Bake at 350 for 30 minutes.

CREAMY BROCCOLI AND TURKEY CASSEROLE

1 pkg. Chicken Rice-a-Roni

3 cups turkey breast, cooked and chopped

2 cups broccoli, cooked and chopped

1 can cream of chicken soup

1 1/2 cup milk

1 cup chicken broth

1/2 cup mayonnaise

1/2 cup celery, chopped

1/2 cup onion, chopped

1 8-oz. can sliced water chestnuts, drained

Mix all ingredients together in a 9x13 dish. Bake at 350 for 30 minutes.

CHICKEN STUFFING PIE

2 celery ribs, chopped

1 medium onion, chopped

3 Tbsp. butter

1 pkg. stuffing mix

1 tsp. poultry seasoning

1 Tbsp. parsley flakes

Salt and pepper to taste

2 eggs, well beaten

2 cans chicken broth

4 cups chicken, cooked and cubed

Saute onions and celery. Combine with remaining ingredients and mix well. Turn into greased 9x13 dish. Bake at 350 for 45 minutes.

151

CHICKEN CASSEROLE PIE

3 cups chicken, cooked and chopped
2 celery ribs, diced
2 carrots, peeled and diced
1 onion, finely diced
1/4 cup butter

1/4 cup flour
2 tsp. chicken bouillon
1 cup water
1 can evaporated milk
1 cup cheese, shredded

Crust: 1 1/2 cups flour
1/2 tsp. baking powder
1 tsp. salt

3 Tbsp. cold butter
1/2 cup milk

Spread chicken in a 9x13 casserole dish. Saute vegetables in butter until tender. Add flour and stir until paste forms. Slowly add water, bouillon, and milk, cooking and stirring until thickened and bubbly. Pour over chicken. Sprinkle with cheese. For crust, sift dry ingredients. Cut in butter to resemble coarse crumbs. Stir in enough milk to form a soft dough. Roll out crust. Lay over casserole. Cut slits in crust. Bake at 350 for 30-40 minutes or until crust is golden brown.

The happiest moments of my life have been the few
which I have passed at home in the bosom of my family.

Thomas Jefferson

SALAMI PENNE BAKE

2 cups penne noodles, cooked

1 quart spaghetti sauce

1/2 pound salami, cubed

1 cup ripe olives, sliced

1 cup mozzarella cheese, shredded

1 cup cheddar cheese, shredded

Spread penne noodles in greased 9x13 pan. Combine salami, olives, and 1/2 cup each of the cheeses. Toss over pasta. Pour spaghetti sauce on top and sprinkle with remaining cheese. Bake at 350 for 30 minutes or until cheese is melted and bubbly.

EGGPLANT PARMESAN

3 eggplants, peeled and thinly sliced

2 eggs, beaten

4 cups seasoned bread crumbs

6 cups spaghetti sauce

16 oz. mozzarella cheese, shredded

1/2 cup Parmesan cheese

1/2 tsp. dry basil

Dip eggplant slices in egg and roll in bread crumbs to coat. Place in greased 9x13 casserole dish. Pour spaghetti sauce over eggplant. Sprinkle with mozzarella and Parmesan cheeses and basil. Bake 375 for 30 minutes

153

Friday has become my favorite night to cook. I'm not sure how it happened, but I think it's because I felt Friday was the night to party. We always made pizza and rented a movie. Without us even realizing it, Friday became our family fun night. We started making other fun foods and often invited friends over. This turned out to be a real blessing in our family, because as our children grew, they seemed to spend a lot of time with their friends in our home. Even through their years in college, they would often arrange parties at our home. We usually played games and these parties often turned into talent nights where friends played the piano or the guitar. My husband and I, being used to being around, stayed around. We always joined in and talked and played games with our children and their friends. We sang songs with them and we felt the bond become so strong with our children and even their friends. This has proven to be such a strength in the lives of our children. I hope you'll enjoy these favorites in your family, too.

I also found Friday to be a night when my children were excited to help make the foods for our parties. Because of this I have chosen to include recipes kids can help with in this section.

Friday

Favorites

and
Cooking with Kids

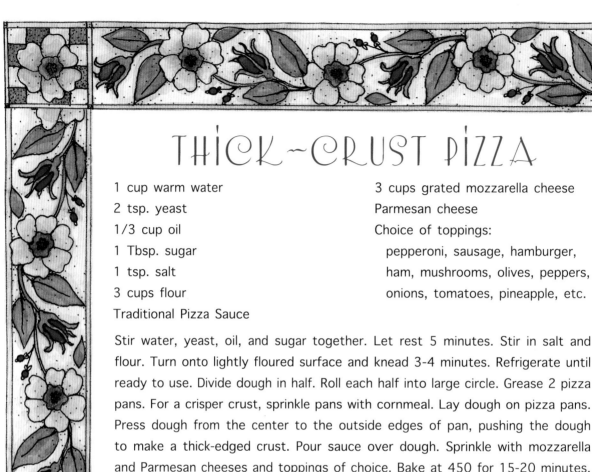

THICK~CRUST PIZZA

1 cup warm water
2 tsp. yeast
1/3 cup oil
1 Tbsp. sugar
1 tsp. salt
3 cups flour
Traditional Pizza Sauce

3 cups grated mozzarella cheese
Parmesan cheese
Choice of toppings:
    pepperoni, sausage, hamburger,
    ham, mushrooms, olives, peppers,
    onions, tomatoes, pineapple, etc.

Stir water, yeast, oil, and sugar together. Let rest 5 minutes. Stir in salt and flour. Turn onto lightly floured surface and knead 3-4 minutes. Refrigerate until ready to use. Divide dough in half. Roll each half into large circle. Grease 2 pizza pans. For a crisper crust, sprinkle pans with cornmeal. Lay dough on pizza pans. Press dough from the center to the outside edges of pan, pushing the dough to make a thick-edged crust. Pour sauce over dough. Sprinkle with mozzarella and Parmesan cheeses and toppings of choice. Bake at 450 for 15-20 minutes, or until crust is golden brown. Slice and serve hot.

THIN AND CRISPY CRUST

Follow above recipe, but add 1 tsp. vinegar to the oil and sugar. Divide dough into 3 parts. Bake according to recipe.

TRADITIONAL PIZZA SAUCE

1 16-oz. can stewed tomatoes
2 Tbsp. sugar

1/4 tsp. garlic powder
1/2 tsp. Italian seasoning

Blend stewed tomatoes, with juice, in the blender until just blended. Combine tomatoes with remaining ingredients in a saucepan. Cook and stir over medium heat until sauce turns deeper red in color. Spread over dough for pizza or use for dipping bread sticks.

GARLIC BREAD STICKS

Follow recipe for Thick-Crust Pizza, but roll dough and place on a large greased cookie sheet. Spread butter over dough. Sprinkle with garlic powder, salt, and Parmesan cheese. If desired, sprinkle with Italian seasoning. Using a pizza cutter, cut 2-inch strips and then cut the strips in half. Bake as directed.

CHEESE~STUFFED STICKS

Follow above instructions, but cut strips 4 inches wide. Sprinkle with Parmesan and mozzarella cheeses. Fold over and seal edges. Butter and season tops as for bread sticks. Bake as directed.

157

FRENCH BREAD PIZZA

1 loaf french bread
2 cups pizza sauce
1/2 cup salsa

2 cups grated cheddar cheese
1 pound hamburger, cooked
1 can ripe olives

Slice French bread loaf as you would a hoagie bun. Turn insides of loaf face up and place on a large baking sheet. Mix pizza sauce and salsa together and spread over both sides of french bread. Sprinkle cheese, hamburger, and olives over sauce. Bake at 350 for 15-20 minutes, or until edges are golden brown. Slice and serve hot.

PIZZA BURGERS

12 hamburger buns
2 cups pizza sauce

2 cups grated mozzarella cheese
Choice of pizza toppings

Open hamburger buns, turning insides face up, and place on a large baking sheet. Spread pizza sauce on buns. Sprinkle with mozzarella cheese and choice of toppings. Bake at 350 for 15-20 minutes or until edges are golden brown. Serve hot.

PERSONAL PIZZA PARTY

2-4 cans refrigerator biscuits
Pizza sauce
2-3 cups grated mozzarella cheese

Choice of toppings:
pepperoni, ham, pineapple,
olives, peppers, mushrooms

Open biscuit cans. Let each child press 2 or more biscuits flat for mini pizza crusts. Place on greased baking pan. Spread sauce on each crust. Let child place toppings of choice on his or her personal pizza. Bake at 400 8-10 minutes or until edges are golden brown.

When children are beginning in the kitchen, they can get items from the pantry and fridge, help set the table, arrange food for serving, and stir some dishes. As they get older, they can open cans, grate cheese, spread sauces, and make juice. During this process, it is helpful to teach them the two parts to making a meal: making the meal and cleaning up after the meal. Children can carry bowls and utensils to the sink, rinse off dishes, wipe counters, and help with after-meal cleanup. This will also help you enjoy the process more because you won't be left with a big mess.

One of my daughters told me that she stopped helping decorate the Christmas tree because I always re-hung the decorations. She thought that she couldn't do it well enough, so she quit. I cringed when she told me this. Without even realizing it, I was damaging her self-worth. Lucky for me, decorating the tree only happens once a year, but we can make this same common mistake in our kitchen . . . every day. Be sure that you recognize that the way the casserole or cake turns out isn't nearly as important as how the child turns out. A nurturing mother will look for ways to build her children's self worth as they are learning new skills.

MEDITERRANEAN PIZZA

1 Thin and Crispy Crust recipe
Garlic Alfredo Pizza Sauce
2 cups mozzarella cheese
1 cup garlic feta cheese

1/2 cup bacon bits
1/2 cup sun-dried tomatoes
1/2 cup cooked spinach
1/2 cup artichoke hearts

Prepare two crusts as directed for Thin and Crispy Crust. Spread sauce over prepared crusts. Sprinkle with cheeses and remaining toppings. Bake at 450 for 10-15 minutes, or until crust is golden brown. Slice and serve hot.

ALFREDO PIZZA SAUCE

2 Tbsp. butter
1 Tbsp. flour

1 cup whipping cream
1/4 tsp. salt

Melt butter in saucepan. Stir in flour. Slowly add cream. Stir until thickened and bubbly. Add salt and mix well. Spread over pizza crust and bake as directed.

For Garlic Alfredo Pizza Sauce, add 1/4 tsp. garlic powder to flour and butter.

GARLIC CHICKEN PIZZA

1 Thin and Crispy Crust recipe
Garlic Alfredo Pizza Sauce
2 cups mozzarella cheese, grated

1 cup chicken, cooked and chopped
2 green onions, chopped

Prepare pizza crust and place on 2 pizza pans. Spread 1/2 cup sauce on each crust. Sprinkle with cheese, chicken, and green onions. Bake at 450 for 20 minutes or until crust is golden brown. Slice and serve hot.

Pizza is a great place to start cooking with children. The tiniest fingers can place pepperoni and olives on top. And the children will think they made the pizza as you pull it out of the oven.

161

NAVAJO TACOS

10-12 fried Quick Fry Bread scones
Refried Beans
1 pound ground beef
1/2 envelope taco seasoning
Grated cheddar cheese

Salsa
Choice of toppings:
lettuce, tomatoes,
onions, peppers,
olives, sour cream

Brown meat and drain fat. Add taco seasoning and mix well. Spread beans over scones. Top with meat, cheese, salsa, and choice of toppings.

QUICK FRY BREAD

3 cups flour
1 Tbsp. baking powder
1 tsp. salt

1/3 cup powdered milk
3 Tbsp. vegetable oil
3/4 cups water + more

Sift dry ingredients together. Add oil and 3/4 cup water and begin stirring. Continue adding water and stirring until mixture forms into a soft dough. Pinch off pieces a little larger than a golf ball. Stretch with your hands to make a flat round circle. Heat oil in deep skillet. Fry shells until edges start to brown. turn and repeat for other side. Remove from oil and place on paper towel to drain.

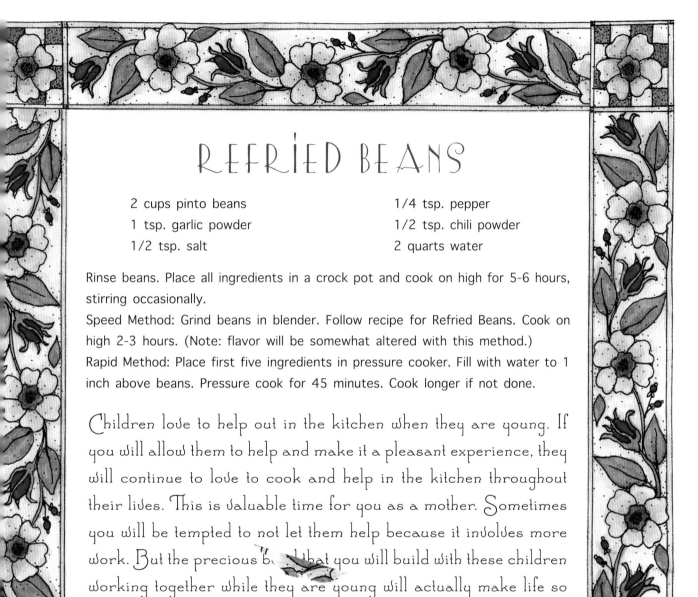

REFRIED BEANS

2 cups pinto beans
1 tsp. garlic powder
1/2 tsp. salt

1/4 tsp. pepper
1/2 tsp. chili powder
2 quarts water

Rinse beans. Place all ingredients in a crock pot and cook on high for 5-6 hours, stirring occasionally.

Speed Method: Grind beans in blender. Follow recipe for Refried Beans. Cook on high 2-3 hours. (Note: flavor will be somewhat altered with this method.)

Rapid Method: Place first five ingredients in pressure cooker. Fill with water to 1 inch above beans. Pressure cook for 45 minutes. Cook longer if not done.

Children love to help out in the kitchen when they are young. If you will allow them to help and make it a pleasant experience, they will continue to love to cook and help in the kitchen throughout their lives. This is valuable time for you as a mother. Sometimes you will be tempted to not let them help because it involves more work. But the precious bond that you will build with these children working together while they are young will actually make life so much simpler throughout those tougher years in their futures.

163

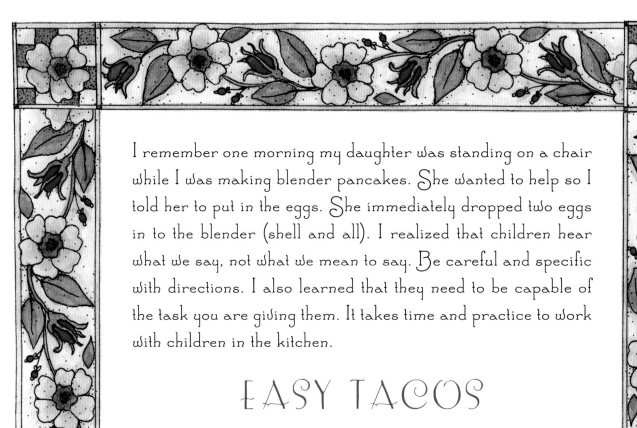

I remember one morning my daughter was standing on a chair while I was making blender pancakes. She wanted to help so I told her to put in the eggs. She immediately dropped two eggs in to the blender (shell and all). I realized that children hear what we say, not what we mean to say. Be careful and specific with directions. I also learned that they need to be capable of the task you are giving them. It takes time and practice to work with children in the kitchen.

EASY TACOS

1 1/2 pounds hamburger
1/2 pkg. taco seasoning
10 flour tortillas
2 cups grated cheddar cheese
Sour cream
Salsa

Choice of toppings:
finely shredded lettuce,
diced tomatoes, onions,
peppers, avocados,
sliced olives

Brown meat and drain fat. Mix with taco seasoning. Heat tortillas in hot skillet with a tiny amount of butter. Keep warm in oven until all tortillas are warmed. Spread desired ingredients inside tortillas and roll up.

164

7~LAYER TACO DIP

1 can refried beans

3 ripe avocados

1 tsp. lemon juice

1/4 tsp. salt

1 cup sour cream

1 Tbsp. taco seasoning

1 cup salsa

2 cups cheese, grated

2 tomatoes, diced

1/4 cup onion, diced

1 cup olives, sliced

Spread beans in a 9x13 casserole dish. Peel and mash 3 avocados. Mix lemon juice and salt with avocados. Spread over beans. Mix sour cream and taco seasoning together. Spread over avocados. Spread salsa over sour cream. Sprinkle grated cheese over salsa. Sprinkle diced tomatoes and onions over cheese. Place sliced olives on top. Serve with tortilla chips.

MINI TOSTADO STACKS

Spread a tiny amount of refried beans on individual round tortilla chips, and place on a serving platter. Prepare toppings of grated cheese, sour cream, salsa, diced onions, peppers, tomatoes, olives, etc. Allow children to place toppings of choice on their personal mini tostado.

Sandwiches are one of the first things that children can learn to make. Let them spread the mayonnaise or fillings. Let them place toppings and the top piece of bread on the sandwiches.

FRENCH BREAD SUBWAY

1 loaf French bread	3 tomatoes, sliced
10 slices sandwich ham	1 red onion, sliced
10 slices turkey breast	Dill pickles, sliced
10 slices cheddar cheese	Mayonnaise or salad dressing
Lettuce leaves	Mustard

Slice French bread lengthwise as you would a hoagie bun. Open loaf with inside facing up. Spread insides with mayonnaise or salad dressing and mustard. Place meats and cheese evenly on bottom side. Place toppings of choice on cheese. Replace top of bread. Cut through loaf diagonally in 2-inch-wide slices.

TUNA SALAD SANDWICHES

3 cans tuna, drained	Lettuce, chopped
3/4 cup Miracle Whip	Tomatoes, chopped

Combine all ingredients. Spread over slices of bread. Top with slices of bread on tuna filling and cut sandwiches in half. Serve with carrot and celery sticks.

166

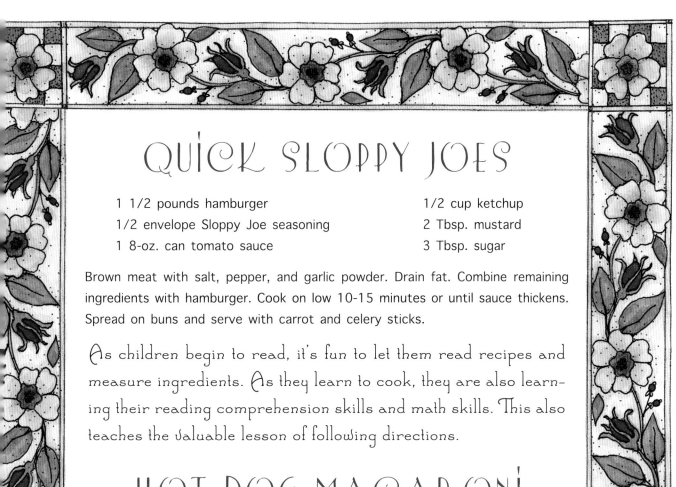

QUICK SLOPPY JOES

1 1/2 pounds hamburger

1/2 envelope Sloppy Joe seasoning

1 8-oz. can tomato sauce

1/2 cup ketchup

2 Tbsp. mustard

3 Tbsp. sugar

Brown meat with salt, pepper, and garlic powder. Drain fat. Combine remaining ingredients with hamburger. Cook on low 10-15 minutes or until sauce thickens. Spread on buns and serve with carrot and celery sticks.

As children begin to read, it's fun to let them read recipes and measure ingredients. As they learn to cook, they are also learning their reading comprehension skills and math skills. This also teaches the valuable lesson of following directions.

HOT DOG MACARONI

1 box macaroni and cheese

5 hot dogs, sliced

Cook macaroni and cheese according to package instructions. In an ungreased skillet, fry sliced hotdogs until both sides are browned. Let a child stir the hotdogs into the macaroni and cheese.

PIGS IN BLANKETS

1 pkg. hot dogs	Ketchup
2 pkgs. refrigerator biscuits	Mustard

Cut hot dogs in half lengthwise. Let child press biscuits flat and wrap around hot dogs so that ends of the hot dog stick out of the dough. Place seam-down on ungreased baking sheet. Bake according to biscuit package directions. Serve with ketchup and mustard.

FISH IN BLANKETS

Follow instructions for Pigs in Blankets, but bake 20 frozen fish sticks at 425 for 10 minutes and allow to cool before wrapping them in the biscuits. Continue and bake as directed as above. Serve with Yummy Fry Sauce or Tartar Sauce.

TARTAR SAUCE

1 cup Miracle Whip	1/3 cup pickle, finely diced
1 Tbsp. vinegar	1 Tbsp. sugar

Mix Miracle Whip, vinegar, pickles, and sugar until well combined. Serve with Fish in Blankets or fish sticks.

168

CORN DOG BITES

1 pkg. hot dogs	3 eggs, well beaten
1/4 cup cornstarch	1/4 cup milk
1/3 cup flour	Ketchup
1/3 cup cornmeal	Mustard
1/2 tsp. salt	

Cut hot dogs in half widthwise. Sift cornstarch, flour, cornmeal, and salt together. Add eggs and milk until well combined. Let child push toothpicks into sides of hotdogs. Dip each hotdog into batter and rotate until well covered. Place a few at a time in hot oil. (Child should not do this part). Rotate corn dog around in hot oil until completely cooked. Remove from oil with a slotted spoon and drain on paper towel. Serve with ketchup and mustard.

MOZZARELLA STICKS

Cut mozzarella cheese as you would French fries. Make batter for Chicken Strips. Push a toothpick into side of cheese and dip in batter. Cook in hot oil, rotating until all sides are cooked. Drain on paper towel.

Deep-Fried Zucchini: Follow above directions using zucchini strips or slices in place of mozzarella cheese. Serve with Yummy Fry Sauce or Tartar Sauce.

CHICKEN STRIPS

1 1/2 pounds boneless, skinless
    chicken strips
1/3 cup cornstarch
1/3 cup flour
3 Tbsp. cornmeal

1 tsp. salt
1/4 tsp. pepper
1/4 cup milk
3 eggs, well beaten
Yummy Fry Sauce

Rinse chicken and pat dry on paper towels. Mix cornstarch, flour, cornmeal, salt, and pepper together. Whisk milk and eggs together in separate bowl. Combine egg mixture with flour mixture until well blended. Pour oil in a deep skillet. Place a matchstick in oil. Heat oil until until match lights. Remove match. Dip chicken strips in batter and drop into hot oil. Cook 5-6 at a time until edges start to brown. Turn chicken pieces and cook until brown. Remove with a slotted spoon and place on paper towel to drain fat. Serve with Yummy Fry Sauce.

YUMMY FRY SAUCE

1 cup Miracle Whip
1/3 cup ketchup

1 Tbsp. yellow mustard

Mix Miracle Whip, ketchup, and mustard until well combined. Serve with Chicken Strips, French Fries, or fish sticks.

170

FRENCH FRIES

6 potatoes, peeled and rinsed   Salt or seasoning
Oil for frying   Yummy fry sauce

Cut potato lengthwise into 1/2-inch thick slices. Hold sliced potato together. Turn potato 1/4 turn and cut lengthwise again into 1/2-inch slices. You should now have fries. Repeat with all potatoes. Rinse fries and pat dry on paper towel. Heat oil as in directions for Chicken Strips. Place cooked fries on paper towel to drain. Immediately sprinkle with salt or seasoning. Serve with ketchup or Yummy Fry Sauce.

BAKED POTATO LOGS

1/4 cup butter, melted   Salt and pepper
6 potatoes, well scrubbed   Seasoned salt

Cut unpeeled potatoes into quarters lengthwise. Cut each quarter in half lengthwise again. Place on greased baking sheet. Brush top side with butter and sprinkle with salt, pepper, and seasoned salt. Bake at 450 for 20 minutes. Remove from oven. Turn potatoes and brush top side with butter and seasoning as before. Bake at 450 for 10 more minutes or until potatoes are tender. Serve with Yummy Fry Sauce.

171

TERIYAKI KABOB STIX

3 lbs. boneless, skinless chicken thighs
2 Tbsp. butter
2 Tbsp. flour
1/4 cup water
1/3 cup brown sugar

1/2 tsp. ground ginger
1/4 tsp. dry mustard
1/4 tsp. garlic powder
1/4 cup soy sauce
Pineapple chunks

Sear both sides of chicken thighs in hot skillet. Fill pan with 1/2 inch water. Cover and simmer chicken 20 minutes or until done. Remove chicken from pan. Add butter and flour to remaining water. Cook and stir until paste forms. Add 1/2 cup water and brown sugar and stir until sugar dissolves. Add remaining ingredients and cook and stir over medium heat until thickened and bubbly. Cut chicken into bite-sized cubes. Return chicken cubes to pan. Stir to coat. Drain pineapple chunks. Let children push their own chicken and pineapple chunks onto kabob skewers. Broil at 500 for 2-5 minutes or until pineapple starts to brown on edges. Cool slightly before eating.

FRIED HAM KABOB STIX

Cut precooked ham into cubes. Fry ham cubes in hot skillet until edges start to brown. Follow above recipe, using fried ham cubes in place of chicken.

172

My sister once told me that it takes a lot of time and attention to work with children when they are young to teach them these new tasks. Sometimes it seems so hard and frustrating, but one day she realized this training was more for her as a mother than it was for her child. She was learning to take time and spend it with her child. If she could train herself now to take time and teach and work with her small child, it would be easier for her to take time and work with her teenaged child. I know my sister is right. A relationship with your teenager doesn't start when she turns thirteen. Don't wait! Start cooking with your kids right now. Don't think of the mess . . . think of the child!

DINNER WAFFLES

1 waffle recipe	1/2 can milk
2 cans tuna, drained	1 cup peas
1 can cream of mushroom soup	Cheese, grated

Make waffles according to directions. Combine remaining ingredients in a medium saucepan. Heat through and serve over waffles. You can substitute hamburger gravy for the tuna gravy.

Saturday is our day for chores. The family works together cleaning the house, mowing the lawn, weeding the garden, and doing other household chores. Sometimes it's nine or ten in the morning before we're thinking about breakfast. In our family it has become a tradition to have Saturday morning brunch when all the chores have been done. Our dad is usually the one who gets things going. He gives everyone an assignment, and soon we have a wonderful morning meal. But truthfully, this recipe collection is designed for every morning, not just for Saturday, because breakfast is the most important meal of the day . . . every day!

I hope you will savor this collection of some of our family's favorite morning recipes, and remember: you don't have to wait until Saturday!

Saturday

Morning Brunch

BREAKFAST PITA POCKETS

1/2 pound sausage

6 slices bacon

1/2 cup onions, diced

1/2 cup green peppers, diced

6 eggs

2 Tbsp. milk

1 cup Colby-Monterrey Jack cheese, shredded

3 pita breads, halved

Cook sausage until well done. Add bacon, onions, and green peppers; cook 4 minutes longer until sausage is heated through and bacon is crisp. Remove and keep warm. Whisk eggs, milk, and salt and pepper to taste. Pour into skillet. Cook and stir over medium heat until eggs are almost set. Add sausage mixture and cheese. Cook and stir for 2 minutes or until eggs are completely set and cheese is melted. Spoon into pita pockets.

SAUSAGE EGG MUFFINS

6 eggs

6 sausage patties

6 English muffins

6 slices cheese

Place a wide-mouthed canning jar lid ring on a hot greased skillet. Crack egg and pour into ring. Hold ring until egg is firm enough that it will not spread outside of the ring. Meanwhile, toast English muffins. Cook sausage until well done. Place sausage, egg, and cheese between muffin halves. Repeat for all muffins.

BEST~EVER HASH BROWNS

4-6 leftover baked potatoes   Salt and pepper
3-4 Tbsp. butter

Peel skins from potatoes. Chop or grate potatoes into a large bowl. Melt butter in skillet or on griddle. Saute potatoes in butter until they become golden and crispy. Sprinkle with salt and pepper. If desired, you can leave the skins on the potatoes for this recipe.
Combine bacon bits with hash browns for country-fried hash browns.

SAGE AND CHEDDAR POTATOES

2 tsp. rubbed sage
1 1/2 tsp. salt
1/2 tsp. ground black pepper
3 pounds potatoes, peeled and thinly sliced

1 large onion, thinly sliced
1 8-oz. pkg. cheddar cheese, grated
1 cup chicken broth
1 cup heavy cream

Mix sage, salt, and pepper in small bowl. Layer one-third of the potatoes and one-half of the onion in lightly greased 13x9 dish. Sprinkle with 1 teaspoon of the sage mixture and one-third of the cheese. Repeat layers, ending with potatoes, sage mixture, and cheese. Stir broth and cream in medium bowl with wire whisk until well blended. Pour evenly over potatoes. Bake in 400 oven 1 hour or until potatoes are tender and top is golden. Let stand 5 minutes before serving.

BREAKFAST QUICHE

Crust:

2 cups flour

1 tsp. salt

1/2 cup butter

8-10 Tbsp. cold water

Sift flour and salt together. Cut in butter. Mix in enough water to form dough. Press dough in greased 9x13 casserole dish. (You can substitute 2 packages refrigerator biscuits for crust.)

Quiche Filling:

8 slices bacon, crumbled

1/3 cup green pepper, diced

1/3 cup onion, chopped

1/3 cup tomato, chopped (opt.)

8 eggs, well beaten

1 cup grated cheddar cheese

1/4 cup milk

Sprinkle bacon and vegetables over crust. Whisk eggs, milk, and salt together. Pour egg mixture over vegetables. Sprinkle cheese on top. Bake at 400 for 30 minutes or until knife inserted comes out clean.

HASH BROWN SAUSAGE BAKE

1 20-oz. pkg. hash browns

1/3 cup butter, melted

1 tsp. beef bouillon granules

1 pound ground pork sausage

1/3 cup onion, chopped

1 cup small-curd cottage cheese

3 eggs, lightly beaten

1 cup cheddar cheese, grated

Combine the hash browns, butter, and bouillon. Press onto the bottom and up the sides of a greased 10-inch pie plate. Bake at 350 for 25-30 minutes or until edges are lightly browned. In a skillet cook sausage and onion over medium heat until meat is no longer pink; drain. Combine the sausage mixture, cottage cheese, eggs, and cheese in bowl. Pour the filling into the crust. Bake at 350 for 40-45 minutes or until a knife inserted comes out clean. Let stand for 5 minutes before cutting.

BREAKFAST CASSEROLE

6 slices bread, lightly toasted

1 1/2 cups cheese, grated and divided

1/2 pound sausage, browned and drained

4 eggs, room temperature

Tear toasted bread and spread evenly in a buttered 9x13 dish. Sprinkle with 1 cup cheese and sausage. Beat together eggs, 3 Tbsp. milk, and mustard. Pour over bread mixture. Sprinkle with salt and pepper. Mix soup and 1/2 cup milk. Pour over top. Bake at 350 for about 1 hour or until eggs are thoroughly cooked. Sprinkle cheese on top during last 20 minutes of baking time.

BREAKFAST IN A BLANKET

5 link sausages, cooked

5 eggs

1 pkg. refrigerator biscuits

5 slices cheese

Fully cook sausage links. Scramble eggs or cook them individually. Press 2 refrigerator biscuits together to make a blanket. Layer the slice of cheese, the egg, and the sausage link in the center of the biscuit. Fold biscuit ends up and then pull sides to center and overlap. Bake, seam-side down, according to biscuit package directions.

KEN'S FAMOUS PANCAKES

2 cups all-purpose flour

1 Tbsp. baking powder

2 Tbsp. sugar

1 tsp. salt

1/4 cup powdered milk

2 eggs

1/4 cup vegetable oil

2 cups water

Mix dry ingredients together. (Ken's secret to perfect pancakes is to fluff the dry ingredients with a wire whisk for a few minutes. Also, if you let the eggs get to room temperature they will make your pancakes lighter.) Beat egg, oil, and milk together until well blended. Pour into dry ingredients and stir just until moist. Drop onto hot oiled griddle. Cook until bubbles appear all over and edges are browned. Flip pancake over and cook other side. (Don't turn pancake more than once, and don't press pancake down.) (Note: You can substitute 2 cups milk for the powdered milk and water.)

WHOLE~WHEAT PANCAKES

Follow above recipe, substituting whole-wheat flour for the all-purpose flour.

BLENDER WHEAT PANCAKES

Blend 1 cup wheat in a blender to get a coarse flour. Add 1 cup milk, 1/4 cup butter, and 2 eggs. Blend until well mixed. Add 1 tsp. salt, 2 Tbsp. sugar or honey, and 1/4 tsp. baking soda. Blend on high until mixed. Pour batter onto hot greased griddle. Cook until bubbles appear all over and edges start to brown. Flip and cook other side.

GERMAN PANCAKE

1/4 cup butter

6 eggs

1 cup milk

1 cup flour

1 tsp. salt

Place butter in 9x13 pan. While pre-heating, place pan in oven to melt butter (don't let it burn). Beat eggs. Stir in milk, flour, and salt. Mix well. Pour batter over melted butter. Bake at 450 for 15-20 minutes or until edges are golden brown.

FRENCH CREPES

1 cup all-purpose flour

1/2 tsp. salt

4 large eggs

2 egg yolks

2 1/2 cups milk

1 Tbsp. vanilla

1/2 cup butter, melted

Sift flour and salt together. Whisk eggs, egg yolks, vanilla, and melted butter together. Add to flour mixture and mix well. Heat and lightly butter or oil small skillet. Use a measuring cup to pour 1/4 cup batter into skillet. Quickly swirl pan to spread batter. Cook until edges are brown. Flip crepe and cook other side. Sprinkle with powdered sugar and roll up.

FRUIT~FILLED CREPES

Follow recipe for French Crepes. For fruit filling, sprinkle 1/4 cup sugar over 1 cup fresh or frozen fruit of choice. Let stand for 15 minutes. Beat 1 cup whipping cream with 1/2 cup powdered sugar and 1 tsp. vanilla until soft peaks form. Spread fruit filling down center of crepes and roll up. Top with whipped cream and a spoonful of fruit.

COTTAGE CHEESE PANCAKES

1 cup cottage cheese

4 large eggs

1/2 cup flour

1/4 tsp. salt

1/4 tsp. baking soda

6 Tbsp. melted butter

Combine cottage cheese and eggs in a blender. Blend until smooth. In a bowl, combine flour, salt, and baking soda. Pour cottage cheese mixture and melted butter into flour mixture and stir well. Pour batter onto hot oiled or buttered griddle in 3- to 4-inch circles. Cook until bubbles appear all over and edges start to brown. Flip and cook other side.

In the cottage there is joy when there's love at home.

STUFFED FRENCH TOAST

1 loaf French bread, unsliced

1 8-oz. pkg. cream cheese, softened

1/3 cup fruit preserves

5 eggs, beaten

1/4 cup milk

1/2 tsp. vanilla

1/4 tsp. ground cinnamon

1/8 tsp. ground nutmeg

2 Tbsp. butter

Powdered sugar

Slice French bread into 1-inch-thick slices. Cut a pocket in each slice by cutting from top crust almost to bottom crust. In a small bowl stir together cream cheese and preserves. Spread about 1 tablespoon cream cheese mixture in each bread pocket. In a shallow dish beat eggs, milk, vanilla, cinnamon, and nutmeg. Dip bread into egg mixture. In large skillet or on griddle cook half of the bread slices in 1 tablespoon of the butter over medium heat for 3-4 minutes or until golden brown, turning once. Repeat with remaining bread slices and butter. Sprinkle with powdered sugar. Serve with chunky fruit topping that will blend with fruit preserves.

HOMEMADE MAPLE SYRUP

2 cups sugar

2 cups water

2 tsp. maple flavoring

2 Tbsp. corn syrup (opt.)

Mix water and sugar in a small saucepan. Bring to a boil, stirring until sugar dissolves. Boil 5 minutes without stirring. If desired, stir in corn syrup. Remove from heat and stir in maple flavoring.

Homemade Fruit Syrup: Follow recipe for Homemade Maple Syrup, but replace maple flavoring with any flavor fruit extract.

CHUNKY PEACH TOPPING

1 29-oz. can sliced peaches, undrained

1/3 cup brown sugar

2 Tbsp. butter

1/3 cup water

Combine all ingredients in saucepan. Mash peaches with potato masher into small chunks. Bring to a boil and let boil for 5 minutes. Remove from heat and cool 5 minutes before serving.
Note: You can substitute other fruit for the peaches in this recipe.

BUTTERMILK SYRUP

1/4 cup butter

1/4 cup flour

1/2 cup sugar

1 cup buttermilk

1 tsp. vanilla

Melt butter in saucepan. Stir in flour and sugar. Add buttermilk and cook and stir over medium heat until sauce thickens. Remove from heat and add vanilla.

LEMON BREAD

1/2 cup vegetable oil

1 cup sugar

2 eggs, well beaten

1/2 cup milk

1 1/2 cups flour

1 tsp. baking powder

1/2 tsp. salt

1 tsp. lemon extract

Blend first 4 ingredients together. Sift dry ingredients together. Blend with egg mixture and stir in lemon extract. Pour into greased loaf pans. Bake at 350 for 30-35 minutes or until knife inserted in center comes out clean. While bread is still hot, prick top all over with toothpick or fork. Pour glaze over top. Remove bread from pan when bread is completely cooled.

Glaze: Stir together 1/4 cup sugar and 1/4 cup lemon juice. Pour over hot bread.

SOUR CREAM SWEET BREAD

1 1/3 cup butter

1 1/2 cups sugar

2 eggs

1 tsp. vanilla

1 cup sour cream

3 cups flour

1 tsp. soda

1 tsp. salt

2 tsp. cinnamon

1 tsp. nutmeg

Cream first five ingredients together. In separate bowl, sift dry ingredients together. Mix dry ingredients with creamed mixture. Pour batter into a greased 9x13 pan. Bake at 350 for 30 minutes or until toothpick inserted in center comes out clean.

184

BANANA NUT BREAD

4 medium bananas
1 tsp. baking soda
1/2 cup vegetable oil
1 cup sugar

2 large eggs
1 1/2 cups flour
1 tsp. salt
1/2 cup walnuts (opt.)

Mash bananas with potato masher until all lumps are gone. Dissolve soda in 2 Tbsp. hot water. Add soda to bananas and stir well. Mix all remaining ingredients into bananas. Add chopped walnuts if desired. Pour into greased 8-inch-square pan. Bake at 350 for 20-30 minutes or until knife inserted in center comes out clean.

BLENDER ZUCCHINI BREAD

1 cup vegetable oil
3 cups zucchini, chopped
3 eggs
2 cups sugar
1 tsp. vanilla
3 cups flour
1 1/2 tsp. baking soda
1 tsp. salt
1 Tbsp. cinnamon

Blend oil and zucchini in blender until pureed. Add egg and vanilla and blend well. Sift dry ingredients into a mixing bowl. Add zucchini mixture and stir well. Pour into two medium greased loaf pans. Bake at 350 for 30-35 minutes or until a knife inserted in center comes out clean.

SPICED PUMPKIN BREAD

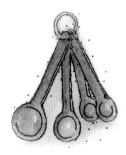

2 cups solid-pack pumpkin
1/2 cup butter, softened
1 cup sugar
2 eggs, well beaten
2 cups all-purpose flour

1 1/2 tsp. baking soda
1/2 tsp. salt
2 tsp. ground cinnamon
1 tsp. ground ginger
1 tsp. ground allspice

Stir first four ingredients until well blended. Sift dry ingredients together. Stir into pumpkin mixture just until moist. Pour batter into two medium greased loaf pans. Bake at 350 for 40-50 minutes or until knife inserted in center comes out clean.

APPLESAUCE BREAD

Follow recipe for Spiced Pumpkin Bread, but replace pumpkin with applesauce. Continue as directed.

APPLESAUCE OR PUMPKIN MUFFINS

Follow recipe for Spiced Pumpkin Bread or Applesauce Bread, but add nuts, raisins, dried cranberries, or chocolate chips as desired, and stir into batter. Pour batter into greased or paper-lined muffin cups rather than loaf pans. Bake at 350 for 20 minutes or until tops are golden brown.

BROWN SUGAR MUFFINS

1/2 cup butter	1 tsp. soda
1 cup brown sugar	1/2 tsp. salt
2 eggs	1 cup milk
1/2 cup raisins (opt.)	1 tsp. vanilla
1/2 cup walnuts (opt.)	2 cups flour

Cream butter, brown sugar, and eggs together. If desired, chop raisins and walnuts and stir into creamed mixture. Add soda and salt and mix well. Stir in milk and vanilla. Add flour and stir just until moist. Pour into greased or paper-lined muffin cups. Bake at 375 for 20 minutes.

RAISIN BRAN MUFFINS

2 eggs, well beaten	1/2 cup vegetable oil
1 cup milk	1/2 tsp. salt
2 tsp. baking soda	1/2 15-oz. box raisin
1 1/2 cups sugar	bran cereal
1/2 cup sour cream	2 cups flour

Mix first seven ingredients together until well blended. Stir raisin bran and flour into wet mixture just until moist. Pour batter into greased or paper lined muffin cups. Bake at 400 for 15 minutes or until tops are golden brown.

A soft answer turneth away wrath. Proverbs 15:1

CRANBERRY MUFFINS

1 cup cranberries
3/4 cup sugar
1/3 cup orange juice
1 3/4 cups flour
3 tsp. baking powder

1 tsp. salt
1 egg
1/2 cup milk
1/3 cup oil

Chop cranberries and mix with orange juice and sugar. Set aside. Sift dry ingredients together. Blend remaining ingredients together. Stir into cranberry mixture. Pour over dry ingredients and stir just until moist. Pour batter into greased or paper-lined muffin cups. Bake at 400 for 20 minutes or until tops are golden brown.

SWEET BLUEBERRY MUFFINS

1 large egg
1/2 cup milk
1/4 cup vegetable oil
1 1/2 cups flour

1/2 cup sugar
2 tsp. baking powder
1/2 tsp. salt
1 cup blueberries

Crumb Topping:
1/2 cup flour
1/2 cup sugar

1/4 cup butter, softened

Combine eggs, milk, and oil. In a separate bowl, sift together flour, sugar, baking powder, and salt. Stir wet ingredients into dry just until moist. Fold in blueberries. Pour batter into greased or paper lined muffin cups, filling 2/3 full. Combine crumb topping ingredients until mixture resembles coarse crumbs. Sprinkle crumb mixture over unbaked muffins. Bake at 400 for 20 minutes or until tops are golden brown.

RASPBERRY STREUSEL MUFFINS

1/2 cup butter

1/2 cup sugar

1 large egg

2 cups flour

1/2 tsp. baking powder

1/2 tsp. baking soda

1/2 tsp. cinnamon

1/4 tsp. salt

1/2 cup milk

1/2 cup sour cream

1 tsp. vanilla

1 cup raspberries,
   fresh or frozen

Powdered sugar

Streusel Topping:

1/2 cup flour

1/2 cup quick oats

1/2 cup sugar

1/2 tsp. cinnamon

1/8 tsp. salt

6 Tbsp. butter

Cream butter and sugar together. Add egg and beat until well blended. Sift dry ingredients together. Stir milk, sour cream, and vanilla into creamed mixture. Pour over dry ingredients and stir just until moist. Fold in raspberries. Pour batter into greased or paper-lined muffin cups. Combine topping ingredients until mixture resembles coarse crumbs. Sprinkle crumb mixture over batter. Bake at 400 for 20 minutes or until tops are golden brown.

APPLE STREUSEL MUFFINS

Follow recipe for Raspberry Streusel Muffins, but add 1/2 teaspoon nutmeg and increase cinnamon to 1 teaspoon. Replace fresh raspberries with 1 cup finely diced apples.

GRANDMA'S CINNAMON ROLLS

2 pkg. active dry yeast
1 Tbsp. sugar
1/2 cup warm water
1 Tbsp. baking powder
1 cup butter
2 cups buttermilk
4 large eggs

2/3 cup sugar
2 tsp. salt
6-7 cups flour
1/2 cup sugar
2 tsp. cinnamon
1/2 cup brown sugar

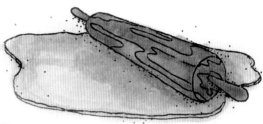

Dissolve yeast and 1 Tbsp. sugar in warm water. Melt butter in saucepan. Stir in buttermilk and eggs. Mix together in a large mixing bowl. Add sugar, salt, and 4 cups flour and beat with mixer until smooth. Stir in enough flour to make a moderately stiff dough. Turn onto floured surface and knead 7-8 minutes. Place in greased bowl and let rest 15 minutes. Divide dough in half. Roll dough to 1/2" thickness. Sprinkle water over dough. Sprinkle with sugar, cinnamon, and brown sugar. Roll dough jelly-roll style. Cut 1/2-inch thick slices. Place on greased baking pan. Let raise until double. Bake at 375 for 20-25 minutes or until edges just start to turn golden. Remove from oven and spread Butter Cream Frosting on rolls immediately.

BUTTER CREAM FROSTING

1/4 cup butter
1/4 cup whipping cream
2 cups powdered sugar
1 tsp. vanilla

Beat butter until creamy. Add whipping cream, vanilla, and enough powdered sugar to make a creamy frosting.

CINNAMON MONKEY BREAD

Dough from Basic White Bread recipe
1 cup butter

1 cup sugar
4 Tbsp. cinnamon

Melt butter. Mix cinnamon and sugar together. Cut dough into 24 pieces. Dip pieces of dough into butter and then into the cinnamon-sugar mixture. Arrange pieces of dough in two greased loaf pans. Cover and let raise until double (about 1 1/2 hours). Bake at 350 for for 25 minutes. Transfer hot bread with syrup into casserole dish to serve.

GLAZED DOUGHNUTS

1 pkg. active dry yeast
1 1/4 cup milk
1/4 cup butter
1 tsp. salt

4 1/2 to 5 cups flour
3/4 cup sugar
1/4 tsp. nutmeg
3 eggs, beaten

Dissolve yeast in 1/4 cup warm water. Melt butter, milk, and salt together in a saucepan. Remove from heat and cool to lukewarm. Add yeast and stir. Pour into a mixing bowl. Gradually add 2 2/3 cups flour, beating thoroughly. Place in warm spot and let stand until full of bubbles. In a separate bowl, combine sugar, nutmeg, and eggs. Pour into dough mixture and mix well. Add remaining flour and knead until well mixed. Cover and let raise in a warm place for about 1 hour.

Turn out onto lightly floured surface and roll to about 1/2-inch thickness. Cut with a doughnut cutter. Let rise on a floured surface until tops are springy when touched. Heat oil. *(Place a match in oil. When the match lights, your oil is hot enough to fry. Remove match before frying doughnuts.)* Deep-fry doughnuts in oil. Place on paper towels to drain excess fat.

Glaze:

Mix 1/2 cup milk, 1 tsp. vanilla, and enough powdered sugar to make a creamy glaze. Glaze doughnuts while hot.

STOVE~TOP GRANOLA

1/3 cup butter
1/3 cup sugar
1/3 cup brown sugar
1/3 cup honey
1/3 cup milk

1/3 cup peanut butter
1 tsp. vanilla
3-4 cups quick oats
3/4 cup raisins (opt.)

Melt butter in medium saucepan. Stir in next four ingredients. Cook and stir over medium heat until mixture starts to boil. Boil for one minute. Remove from heat and stir in peanut butter, vanilla, oats, and raisins (optional).

Oven-Toasted Granola:
Spread Stove-Top Granola on a large cookie sheet. Bake at 450 for 10 minutes. Turn mixture and bake additional 10 minutes or until lightly toasted.

FRUIT AND NUT CEREAL

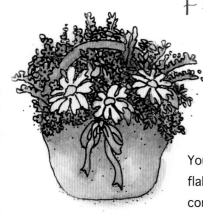

1 18-oz. box corn flakes
1/4 cup melted butter
1/3 cup honey or brown sugar
1/2 cup coconut (opt.)

1 cup craisins or raisins
or other dried fruits
1 cup toasted almonds,
chopped

You can use any variety of fruits and nuts for this recipe. Spread corn flakes on large cookie sheet. Combine remaining ingredients. Pour over corn flakes. Bake at 400 for 10 minutes.

CHEWY GRANOLA BARS

2/3 cup honey
1/4 cup brown sugar
1 cup peanut butter
1 1/2 cups granola

1 1/2 cups crispy rice cereal
1/2 cup sliced almonds or
      finely chopped peanuts
1/2 cup flaked coconut

Combine honey and brown sugar in a medium saucepan. Cook and stir over medium heat until bubbly. Remove from heat. Stir in peanut butter until well blended. Mix remaining ingredients. Add to peanut butter mixture and mix well. Press into ungreased 9x13 baking pan. Chill 1 hour. Cut into bars.

The voice of parents is the voice of Gods,

for to their children they are heaven's lieutenants.

William Shakespeare

193

Favorite recipes

No success can compensate for failure in the home.

David O. McKay

My grandmother's sister Lila Keller was a very gracious woman. She was also an expert on etiquette. She was frequently asked to speak on the subject of table manners. She once said, "The reason our youth don't know their table manners is because nobody eats around the dinner table any more. They just sit in front of the television and shovel in the food without thinking of their behavior." I have been taught that it's proper to serve the salad first. But my husband met a woman from Italy who told him Americans eat backwards. She informed him that we should eat salad last so the salad greens will help digest the food. I'm not trying to change what is usual in our culture, and I certainly believe in table manners, but I saved salad for last because I think salads are light and easy. Saturday is always my busiest day of the week, so I welcome light and easy!

I hope you will enjoy these salad recipes. I also hope you will remember to eat them around the dinner table, because your children will be grateful if they have been taught simple table manners.

Saturday Night

Salad Bar

GREEK PASTA SALAD

1 12-oz. pkg. spiral rainbow pasta, cooked and drained
1 cup mayonnaise
1 cup Italian dressing
1 cup plum or cherry tomatoes, halved
1 cucumber, peeled and chopped
1 cup ripe black olives, halved
1 cup pimiento-stuffed green olives, halved
1 cup feta cheese, sun-dried tomato-basil flavor

Cook pasta according to package directions. Drain. Combine mayonnaise and Italian dressing in a large mixing bowl. Stir in remaining ingredients. Fold in cooked pasta.

ITALIAN PASTA SALAD

Follow recipe for Greek Pasta Salad, but add 1/4 cup Parmesan cheese with the mayonnaise and Italian dressing. Add 1/2 cup chopped pepperoni slices and 2 cups garlic croutons.

SUMMER PASTA SALAD

1 16-oz. pkg. rainbow pasta
1 cup tomatoes, chopped
1 cup green pepper, chopped
1 cucumber, peeled and chopped
1/2 bottle McCormick's Salad Supreme

1 can ripe olives, sliced
2 eggs, hard-boiled and chopped
1 cup cheddar cheese, cubed
1 bottle Italian salad dressing

Cook pasta according to package directions. Drain. Mix remaining ingredients in a large salad bowl. Fold in pasta until well coated. Chill at least one hour before serving.

PINEAPPLE CHICKEN SALAD

1 cup salad dressing
2 Tbsp. sugar
2 Tbsp. brown sugar
2 cups cooked and cubed
   chicken breasts

2 green onions chopped
1 can crushed pineapple (drained)
2 ribs celery finely diced
1 cup dried cranberries
1 12-oz. pkg. rainbow pasta

Mix first three ingredients; stir until sugar dissolves. Mix remaining ingredients together except pasta. Stir well. Cook pasta according to package directions and fold into dressing.

TUNA MACARONI SALAD

1 8-oz. pkg. elbow macaroni

1 cup mayonnaise

1 Tbsp. vinegar

2 Tbsp. yellow mustard

1 6-oz. can tuna, drained

1 Tbsp. celery seed

1/2 cup onion, diced

1/2 cup celery, diced

1 10-oz. pkg. frozen peas

Salt and pepper

Cook macaroni according to package directions. Drain. In a large bowl, combine remaining ingredients. Season with salt and pepper to taste. Fold in macaroni. If desired, sprinkle with paprika.

BACON MACARONI SALAD

Follow recipe for Tuna Macaroni Salad, but replace the tuna with 10 slices bacon, cooked and crumbled. Replace frozen peas with 1 cup chopped broccoli.

TURKEY MACARONI SALAD

Follow recipe for Tuna Macaroni Salad, but replace tuna with 1 cup cooked and cubed turkey meat. Add 1/2 cup chopped pickles.

BOWTIE BROCCOLI SALAD

1 12-oz. pkg. bowtie pasta
1 bunch broccoli, chopped
1 head cauliflower, chopped
8 slices bacon, cooked and crumbled

1 medium onion, diced
1 cup mayonnaise
1/4 cup Parmesan cheese
1/2 cup Italian dressing

Cook bowtie pasta according to package directions. Drain. Break broccoli and cauliflower into small florets. In a large bowl, combine remaining ingredients. Fold in vegetables and pasta.

SPAGHETTI SALAD

1 7-oz. pkg. spaghetti or angel hair pasta
3/4 cup green pepper, chopped
3/4 cup red pepper, chopped
2-3 green onions, chopped
1 cup tomato, chopped

1 cup zucchini, chopped
1/2 cup Italian dressing
1/4 cup Parmesan cheese
1 Tbsp. parsley flakes
1 Tbsp. sugar

Cook pasta according to package directions. Drain. Combine remaining ingredients together. Fold in pasta until well coated. Allow to sit 1 hour before serving.

HOT CHICKEN SALAD

2 cups chicken, cooked and cubed

2 cups celery, diced

1/2 cup almonds, chopped and toasted

1 20-oz. can pineapple tidbits

1 cup mayonnaise

1/2 tsp. salt

1 tsp. lemon juice

Chow mein noodles

Drain pineapple. Combine with remaining ingredients in a casserole dish. Sprinkle noodles over top. Bake at 400 for 15 minutes. Serve warm.

HAWAIIAN HAYSTACKS

4 cups rice, cooked

2 boneless chicken breasts

1 tsp. chicken bouillon

1 cup water

1/4 tsp. paprika

1 can cream of chicken soup

2 cups milk

Cheddar cheese, grated

Chow mein noodles

Choice of toppings:

onions, celery, tomatoes

olives, pineapple, peas, etc.

Place chicken, bouillon, and water in saucepan. Sprinkle with paprika. Cover and cook until chicken is tender. Remove chicken and chop. Stir soup and milk into chicken broth. Return cubed chicken to pan. Layer haystacks with rice, noodles, gravy, cheese, and your choice of toppings.

202

CHILI TACO SALAD

1 15-oz. can chili con carne
1 16-oz. can stewed tomatoes
1 cup mild or medium salsa
3 cups lettuce leaves, torn
1 cucumber, peeled and chopped
1 16-oz. can whole-kernel corn

2 tomatoes, chopped
1/2 onion, finely diced
2 cups cheese, shredded
Sour cream
1 can black olives
Corn chips

Combine chili beans, stewed tomatoes, and salsa in a saucepan. Cook over medium heat until warmed through. Put remaining ingredients in serving dishes so everyone can make their own salad.

CHEF'S SALAD

1 8-oz. pkg. sliced American cheese
1 8-oz. pkg. sliced provolone cheese
1 8-oz. pkg. sandwich ham slices
3 eggs, hard-boiled and chopped
3 cups lettuce leaves, torn

2 tomatoes, diced
2 cucumbers,
     peeled and diced
1 bottle French
     dressing

Cut cheeses and ham into 1/2x2-inch strips. Toss cheeses, ham, and eggs with vegetables. Fold in French dressing until well coated.

203

SUMMER SQUASH SALAD

2 cups summer squash, sliced

1 cup fresh green beans

2 cups cherry tomatoes

1/2 red onion, sliced

Italian dressing

Boil squash for 1 minute. Remove squash with slotted spoon and place in ice water to crispen. Boil green beans until tender. Remove with slotted spoon and place in ice water to crispen. Toss squash and beans with remaining ingredients.

Eat together when possible, and have meaningful mealtime discussions.
Elder Robert D. Hales

SPINACH SALAD

4 slices bacon, cooked and crumbled

1/4 cup cider vinegar

2 Tbsp. vegetable oil

2 tsp. yellow mustard seed

1/4 cup red onion, sliced

1 tsp. sugar

1 large bunch spinach

3 eggs, hard-boiled and chopped

Cook and crumble bacon. Combine bacon with next five ingredients. Tear spinach leaves. Combine all ingredients and serve immediately.

204

CHINESE CHICKEN SALAD

2 cups chicken breast, cooked and cubed

3 green onions, chopped

2 Tbsp. sesame seeds

1 can Chinese noodles

1 head romaine lettuce

2 cans mandarin oranges, drained

2 Tbsp. sugar

Salt and pepper

1/2 tsp. chicken
    bouillon

2 Tbsp. vinegar

1/4 cup oil

Toss first six ingredients in salad bowl. Blend remaining ingredients for dressing. Pour dressing over salad and stir until well coated. Serve immediately.

PARMESAN SALAD

1 cup mayonnaise

1/4 cup Parmesan cheese

1/4 cup sugar

6-8 slices bacon, cooked well and crumbled

1 head broccoli, chopped

1 head cauliflower, chopped

1 medium onion, finely chopped

Combine first three ingredients. Stir in bacon and vegetables until well coated.

APPLE BROCCOLI SALAD

1/2 cup mayonnaise

3 Tbsp. honey

1 Tbsp. apple cider vinegar

4 cups fresh broccoli florets

2 cups chopped apple

1/2 cup celery, finely diced

1/2 cup raisins

1/4 cup walnuts, chopped

Mix first three ingredients. Chop broccoli, apple, and celery. Add remaining ingredients to mayonnaise mixture and mix until well coated.

AVOCADO CRAB SALAD

1 6-oz. can crab meat, drained

1/3 cup celery, chopped

3 eggs, hard-boiled

2 Tbsp. pimiento

2 Tbsp. onion, chopped

Salt and pepper

1/2 cup mayonnaise

Lemon juice

3-4 small ripe avocados

3 Tbsp. bread crumbs

2 Tbsp. Parmesan cheese

1 Tbsp. butter, melted

3 Tbsp. slivered almonds

Mix first seven ingredients. Cut unpeeled avocados lengthwise in half. Remove pits. Brush avocados with lemon juice and place in casserole dish. Fill avocados with crab meat filling. Mix bread crumbs, cheese, and melted butter together. Sprinkle over avocados and bake at 400 for 10 minutes. Sprinkle with almonds and bake additional 5 minutes.

MOZZARELLA SALAD

4 large tomatoes, cut into wedges

2 cucumbers, peeled and chopped

pound mozzarella cheese, cubed

3 cups romaine lettuce leaves, torn

1 cup craisins

1/2 cup walnuts, chopped

Red Poppy Seed Dressing

Combine all ingredients except dressing in large salad bowl. Pour dressing on just before serving.

Red Poppy Seed Dressing:
3 Tbsp. grape juice concentrate
1 Tbsp. vinegar
3 Tbsp. vegetable oil

3 Tbsp. sugar
2 tsp. poppy seeds
3/4 cup water

Mix all ingredients and stir until sugar is dissolved. Mix just before serving.

TOMATO BREAD SALAD

5 cups garlic croutons

3 cucumbers, peeled and chopped

3 tomatoes, chopped

1/2 red onion, thinly sliced

1/2 cup black olives, sliced

Italian dressing

Parmesan cheese

Parsley flakes

Toss ingredients and serve immediately.

FRUIT~N~YOGURT SALAD

1 16-oz. bag frozen berries

1/2 cup sugar

1 20-oz. can pineapple, drained

4 bananas, peeled and thinly sliced

4 cups vanilla yogurt

1/2 cup powdered sugar

1 tsp. vanilla

Granola (opt.)

In a large mixing bowl, combine frozen fruit with 1/2 cup sugar. Add pineapple and bananas and mix well. In a separate bowl, combine yogurt, powdered sugar, and vanilla. Stir yogurt mixture into fruit. If desired, sprinkle individual servings with granola.

WALDORF SALAD

1 cup apples, diced

1 cup celery, diced

1 cup red grapes, halved

1/2 cup walnuts, chopped

1/4 cup flaked coconut (opt.)

1/4 cup powdered sugar

1/4 cup whipping cream

1/2 cup mayonnaise

In a large mixing bowl, combine first four ingredients. If desired, stir in coconut. Beat powdered sugar and whipping cream together until soft peaks form. Stir in the mayonnaise. Add cream mixture to fruit and stir until well coated. Cover and refrigerate until ready to serve.

WINTER FRUIT SALAD

4 oranges, peeled and diced

4 green apples, chopped

4 bananas, thinly sliced

2 Tbsp. lemon juice

1/2 cup sour cream

1/3 cup honey

Mix first three ingredients. Sprinkle with lemon juice. Mix sour cream and honey. Combine honey mixture with chopped fruit until well coated.

COCONUT FRUIT SALAD

2 cans mandarin oranges, drained

1 can pineapple tidbits, drained

2 peaches, peeled and chopped

1 cup strawberries, sliced

1/2 cup flaked coconut

1 cup whipped topping

1/2 cup nuts, chopped

Combine all ingredients. Cover and refrigerate until ready to serve.

In a world of turmoil and uncertainty, it is more important than ever to make our families the center of our lives and the top of our priorities.

Elder L. Tom Perry

209

Many years ago I was watching my kids play with their cousins while we were at a family gathering. I realized that these people--their cousins, aunts, uncles, and especially their grandparents--were a huge influence in their lives. I knew right then that strengthening extended family ties would also strengthen my children. I realized that as they grew older, they would be faced with difficult choices. And somehow, in that moment, I could see that these family bonds would help keep them strong.

Whether it's a baby blessing, baptism, missionary farewell, or homecoming, we want to share these times with our family. We also like to get together for birthdays, holidays, family reunions, and other special occasions. At times like these, planning a meal can be a big job.

This section has been put together with the extended family in mind. It is my favorite section, because the recipes come from my favorite people. I hope that you will enjoy these recipes. But even more, I hope you will have great family gatherings like we do... and if you have food like this, I'm sure you will!

Extended

Family Gatherings

This Norwegian stew has been served on Christmas Eve since I was a little girl. Thanks to my older brother Dave, this tradition hasn't died. We continue to have Lobscouse at our family Christmas party each year. Serving family recipes like this one is a great way to carry on family traditions.

BEEF LOBSCOUSE

2 pounds bacon, chopped

5- to 6-pound beef roast

2- to 3-pound pork roast

3-4 pounds onions, chopped

10 pounds potatoes, chopped

Salt and pepper

In a 12-quart stew pot, cook chopped bacon until almost crisp. Saute onions in bacon fat. Cut beef and pork roasts into bite-sized chunks. Add meat chunks and stir to brown edges. Cook in meat's own juices for 2-3 hours over low heat. Rinse peeled potatoes and chop into large chunks. Add to meat and stir well. Cover potatoes with water. Cover and cook over low heat, stirring every 30-45 minutes. When potatoes are near tender, stir in salt and pepper to taste. Continue cooking until potatoes are very tender and meat falls apart (total cooking time is approximately 6 hours). Serve with horseradish and ketchup.

Dave Gilgen

CROWD SPAGHETTI SAUCE

3 pounds ground beef
3 pkgs. Hillshire Farms hot link sausages
3 Tbsp. garlic, freshly minced
3 medium onions, finely diced
3 jumbo-sized jars Prego spaghetti sauce
  (Sam's Club or Costco)

3 8-oz. cans tomato paste
Salt and pepper to taste
Basil to taste
Oregano to taste
1/3 cup sugar

In a skillet, brown ground beef with diced onions. Season with salt, pepper, basil, and oregano. Cook until meat is done and onions are translucent. Set aside. Pour spaghetti sauce into a large soup pot. Add tomato paste, salt, pepper, basil, oregano, and sugar to sauce. Peel skins from sausages. Cut in half lengthwise, then cut into ½-inch slices. Brown sausages with 1 tsp. minced garlic. Add remaining garlic to sauce. Stir browned beef and sausages into sauce. Simmer on low, stirring occasionally, for at least 1 hour before serving.

Kodi Gilgen

When preparing spaghetti for a crowd, plan 1 oz. of uncooked spaghetti per person, plus a little extra for seconds. Cook and drain according to package directions. Just before serving, place cooked noodles in large pot of hot tap water. Serve noodles with tongs or slotted spoon, draining excess water before placing pasta on plates. Serve with Crowd Spaghetti Sauce. Prepare toasted garlic bread and ask guests to bring a variety of green salads.

213

BAKED POTATO BAR

Bake enough potatoes for everyone who will attend the gathering. Ask individuals or families to bring toppings, such as:

Butter	Green onions
Sour cream	Broccoli
Grated cheese	Green peas
Cheese Sauce	Hamburger Gravy
Chili Cheese Sauce	Chili con carne
Ranch dressing	Bacon bits

HAMBURGER GRAVY

10 pounds lean ground beef
1 tsp. garlic powder
1 cup flour

2 quarts milk
1 28-oz. can cream of
   mushroom soup

Brown ground beef with garlic powder, then salt and pepper to taste. Do not drain fat. Stir in flour until well blended. Slowly add milk. Cook and stir over medium heat until thickened and bubbly. Stir in cream of mushroom soup. If necessary, add more milk. Heat through. Serve over baked potatoes.

CHEESE SAUCE

1/4 cup butter, melted
1/2 cup flour
4 cups milk

1 8-oz. pkg. Velveeta cheese
2 cups cheddar cheese, grated
1/2 tsp. salt

Stir melted butter and flour until smooth. Slowly add milk. Cook and stir over medium heat until thickened and bubbly. Cut Velveeta cheese into small chunks. Add cheeses and salt to creamy sauce. Cook and stir over medium heat until cheese is melted. Serve over broccoli or baked potatoes. This sauce can also be used for macaroni and cheese.

CHILI CHEESE SAUCE

2 10-oz. cans Ro-Tel diced tomatoes and green chilies
2 12-oz. packages Velveeta cheese

Combine ingredients together in a microwave-safe bowl. Microwave on high for 2 minutes. Remove and stir. Microwave on high for another 2 minutes. Remove and stir. Repeat as necessary until all the cheese is melted and sauce is smoothly blended. Serve over baked potatoes or with tortilla chips.

This is my favorite baked potato topping, and it is really simple to make.

Julie Cline

TERIYAKI CHICKEN ROLLS

6 boneless, skinless chicken breasts

1/3 cup cornstarch

1 cup ketchup

1 cup brown sugar

1 tsp. ground ginger

1 tsp. dry mustard

1 tsp. garlic powder

1/2 cup soy sauce

Place chicken in crock pot. Combine remaining ingredients except cornstarch with 1 quart water and stir well. Pour over chicken. Cook on high 3-4 hours, rotating chicken to bottom so it will marinate. Remove chicken and shred. Return to pot. Add cornstarch and stir well. Cook without lid until sauce is thickened and bubbly, stirring often. Serve on hard rolls or buns.

Kathy Beals

SLOPPY JOES FOR CROWD

8 pounds hamburger

2 envelopes Sloppy Joe seasoning

2 carrots, peeled and shredded

4 stalks celery, finely chopped

2 onions, finely chopped

2 cups ketchup

1/2 cup mustard

3/4 cup sugar

3 29-oz. cans tomato sauce

4 dozen hamburger buns

Cook hamburger with salt, pepper, and garlic powder until browned. Drain fat. Put in a crock pot. Add remaining ingredients and stir well. Cook on high 2-3 hours or on low 4-5 hours. Serve on hamburger buns.

216

BARBECUE BEEF BUNS

2 pounds bacon, chopped
8-9 pounds beef roast
5 pounds pork roast
3 medium onions, chopped
1/4 cup Worcestershire sauce

2 cups brown sugar
3 cups ketchup
1/3 cup yellow mustard
2 cups barbecue sauce
Sliced buns or hard rolls

Cook chopped bacon until almost crisp. Saute onions in bacon fat. Place roasts, bacon, and onions in roasting pan. Cover and bake at 350 for 3 hours. Pour 1 quart water in pan. Cover and bake at 350 for 2 additional hours. Remove from oven. Use a fork in one hand to hold the meat while shredding it with a knife in the other hand. After meat is shredded, add remaining ingredients except buns and stir well. Return to oven. Bake at 350 for an additional 45 minutes or until sauce is bubbly. Serve on sliced buns or rolls. Serves about 60.

This recipe can also be prepared in electric roasting pans. Follow above cooking directions, checking bottom of roasting pans often, and adjusting temperature to prevent burning. If desired, this recipe can also be prepared without the bacon.

217

Barbecues are a great idea for large family gatherings. Grill any of the following recipes, or ask individuals to bring their own meat to grill.

BARBECUED BUTTER CHICKEN

Chicken pieces, with bone and skin
Butter, melted (1-2 Tbsp. per chicken piece)

Rosemary sprigs, fresh

Place chicken pieces on hot grill, skin side down. Using the rosemary sprigs as a baster, baste tops (inside) of chicken with melted butter. Continue cooking and basting each piece until chicken starts to bleed out the bone. Turn chicken pieces over. Using tongs, pull skin off chicken. Baste tops of chicken with rosemary sprigs and melted butter. Repeat basting a few times until chicken is done.

Tom Gilgen

BEST BARBECUED STEAKS

The most important step to great barbecued steaks is choosing a good steak. My favorite is a T-bone or Porterhouse steak. When choosing steaks, look for marbling (white streaks of fat) in the meat. Place steaks on a hot grill. Sprinkle with salt and pepper. As soon as steak starts to bleed, flip it over. As soon as it starts to sweat, take it off.

Tom Gilgen

BARBECUED TURKEY

10 pounds turkey breast, cut up

1 quart 7-up soda pop

2 cups vegetable oil

2 cups soy sauce

1 tsp. garlic powder

1/4 tsp. horseradish (opt.)

Combine all ingredients together in large container with tight fitting-lid. Marinate 24 hours, stirring occasionally. Grill both sides of turkey until browned.

Another simple idea for family gatherings is to ask everyone to bring a favorite one-dish meal. This could be a casserole or crockpot dish. Order or bake dinner rolls to serve with the main dishes.

EASY BARBECUE CHICKEN

1 18-oz. bottle KC Barbecue Sauce (original)

1 18-oz. bottle Red Bull Barbecue Sauce (original)

2 pounds boneless, skinless chicken breasts

Mix the two bottles of barbecue sauce in a crock pot. Cook on high for 20 minutes. Cut chicken into 2-inch strips; stir into the sauce. Cook on low for 3-4 hours or until chicken is tender.

Denan Cox

219

EASY PORK RIBS

2 pounds boneless pork ribs   3 cups water
1/3 cup Au Jus mix

In a skillet, brown all sides of pork ribs. Combine Au Jus mix and water in a crock pot until dissolved. Add browned boneless ribs. Cook on high for 30 minutes. Reduce heat to low and cook 3 hours.

Denan Cox

STUFFED SHELLS AND SAUCE

1 12-oz. pkg. jumbo shells   1 1/2 cups spinach, chopped
1 16-oz. container cottage cheese   1 pound hamburger, browned
1 8-oz. pkg. cream cheese   1 Tbsp. dried basil
2 cups mozzarella cheese, grated   1 Tbsp. dried oregano
3/4 cup Parmesan cheese, grated   1 tsp. minced garlic
1 Tbsp. fresh parsley, chopped   4 8-oz. cans tomato sauce
3/4 tsp. dried basil   1/2 cup mozzarella cheese

Cook shells and drain. Combine the next 7 ingredients and set aside. Combine meat, spices, and tomato sauce in saucepan. Simmer 10 minutes. Spread 1 cup sauce in a 9x13 dish. Fill shells with cheese mixture and arrange in dish. Pour remaining sauce over shells. Bake at 350 for 20 minutes. Sprinkle with remaining cheese. Bake 10 minutes more or until cheese is melted and bubbly.

Kathy Beals

SALSA CHICKEN

6 boneless, skinless chicken breasts

2 16-oz. bottles salsa

1 cup sour cream (opt.)

2 cups cheese, shredded

Place chicken breasts in crock pot. Pour salsa over chicken. Cook on high 3 hours or until chicken is tender. If desired, spread sour cream over top and sprinkle with shredded cheese. Cook additional 30 minutes. Serve over rice.

Kimm Harman

MUSHROOM CHICKEN

6 chicken breast halves

10 large mushrooms, sliced

1 medium sweet onion, sliced

3 Tbsp. butter

2 Tbsp. beef bouillon

2 Tbsp. cornstarch

2 cups cold water

6 slices Monterrey Jack cheese

Season chicken with Lawry's Perfect Blend seasoning. Grill chicken breasts. Meanwhile, saute onions and mushrooms in butter until onions are tender. Combine bouillon, cornstarch, and water in a saucepan until well blended. Cook and stir over medium heat until gravy thickens. Stir in 1/4 of the mushrooms and onions. When chicken is thoroughly cooked, place in a 9x13 pan. Top with sauteed mushrooms and onions and cover with cheese slices. Broil on low until cheese barely melts. Pour gravy over top and serve.

Diane Kunz

CHICKEN TETRAZZINI

3 chicken breasts, cut into 1-inch strips
1 14.5-oz. pkg. Barilla spaghetti
6 oz. mushrooms, sliced
3 Tbsp. butter
Sauce:
3 Tbsp. butter
2 Tbsp. flour
2 1/2 cups chicken broth
1/8 tsp. nutmeg

1 Tbsp. lemon juice
3/4 cup Parmesan cheese
Paprika

1 1/2 tsp. salt
1/2 tsp. pepper
1 cup heavy cream

Grill chicken and cut into bite-sized pieces. Cook spaghetti according to package directions. Drain. Turn into a 9x13 dish. Fold in grilled chicken. Saute mushrooms in butter with lemon juice. Toss with spaghetti and chicken. For sauce, melt butter and flour together in a saucepan. Add broth, seasonings, and cream. Cook and stir until sauce thickens slightly. Stir into chicken, spaghetti, and mushrooms. Mixture will appear soupy, but liquid will be absorbed. Sprinkle with Parmesan cheese and paprika. Bake at 400 for 25 minutes or until browned and bubbly.

Kimm Harman

222

HONEY GINGER CHICKEN

4 chicken breasts, cut into 1-inch strips

1/3 cup ketchup

1/3 cup honey

1 tsp. ground ginger

Grill chicken strips in large skillet. Combine remaining ingredients and pour over grilled chicken. Simmer 10 minutes. Serve over rice.

George Gilgen

CHICKEN AND RICE

4 chicken breasts, cut into 1-inch strips

2 cups long-grain rice, cooked

1 4-oz. can diced green chilies

1 can cream of chicken soup

1 1/2 cups sour cream

4 oz. cheddar cheese, grated

4-oz. Pepper Jack cheese, grated

Cook rice according to package directions. Grill chicken strips in large skillet. Cut chicken into bite-sized pieces. In a 9x13 dish, combine chicken and rice with green chilies, soup, and sour cream. Sprinkle cheeses on top. Bake at 350 for 30 minutes or until cheese is melted.

This is one of the best dishes you will ever eat in your whole entire life!

George Gilgen

CHICKEN PIE DELUXE

2 cups chicken, cooked and diced

1/2 cup milk

2 Tbsp. parsley, chopped

Salt and pepper to taste

Dressing:

1 1/2 cups stuffing (or bread crumbs)

1/2 cup butter, melted

1 can cream of chicken soup

1 can cream of celery soup

1 Tbsp. onion, minced

3/4 cup frozen peas

Dash of onion

Dash of sage

Combine first 8 ingredients in a 9x13 dish. Cover with dressing. Bake at 300 for 30 minutes or until hot and bubbly.

Ann Harman

TURKEY CASSEROLE

3 cups turkey, cooked and shredded

1 bag frozen broccoli

1 can cream of mushroom soup

1/3 soup can milk

2 cups cheese, grated

1 pkg. Stove Top Stuffing

Cover bottom of 9x13 dish with turkey. Cook broccoli. Spread over turkey. Mix soup with milk. Pour evenly over turkey and broccoli. Sprinkle cheese over top. Prepare Stove Top Stuffing according to package directions and spread over casserole. Bake at 350 for 20 minutes.

Ann Harman

224

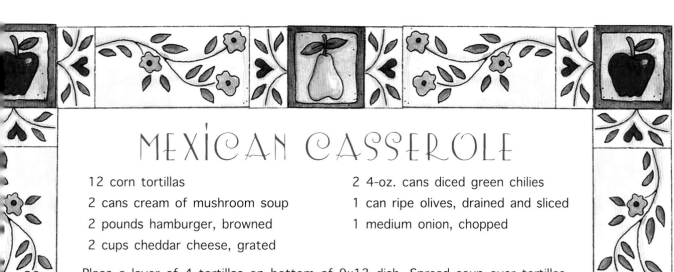

MEXICAN CASSEROLE

12 corn tortillas
2 cans cream of mushroom soup
2 pounds hamburger, browned
2 cups cheddar cheese, grated

2 4-oz. cans diced green chilies
1 can ripe olives, drained and sliced
1 medium onion, chopped

Place a layer of 4 tortillas on bottom of 9x13 dish. Spread soup over tortillas. Sprinkle with meat, cheese, chilies, olives, and onions. Beginning with tortillas, repeat layers twice. Bake at 350 for 30-45 minutes or until bubbly. Serve with salsa and sour cream.

Sandi Stokes

TATER TOT CASSEROLE

1 pound hamburger, browned
1 can cream of mushroom soup
1 cup sour cream
1 1/2 cups cheddar cheese, shredded

1/2 cup milk
Salt and pepper to taste
4 cups tater tots

Combine first 5 ingredients in a 9x13 dish, reserving 1/2 cup cheese to top the casserole. Stir in 3 cups tater tots to mixture. Pour into casserole dish. Top with remaining tater tots and cheese. Cook at 350 for 30-35 minutes or until cheese is melted and tater tots are golden brown.

Bridger Gilgen

225

Soup in bread bowls is a delicious idea on a chilly day. Ask guests to bring a pot of soup, and you provide the bread bowls. You can order them from your bakery or use the recipe in this section to make homemade bread bowls.

CROWD CLAM CHOWDER

5 pounds potatoes
3/4 cup butter
1 onion, finely diced
3 ribs celery, finely diced
3/4 cup flour

2 quarts milk
2 bottles clam juice
4 6-oz. cans diced clams
   (undrained)
Salt and pepper

Peel, chop, and rinse potatoes. Steam potatoes until not quite fork-tender. Meanwhile, in a separate pan, melt butter. Saute onions until they start to go clear. Add celery and saute until soft. Stir in flour to make a roux. Slowly add milk. Add potatoes to milk, and salt and pepper to taste. Cook on medium heat, stirring often. Watch closely; don't let it boil. Continue cooking until potatoes are completely cooked. Add clam juice and mix well. Add diced clams with juice just before serving. Heat through. Salt and pepper to taste.

DeeAnne Gilgen

CREAMY CHICKEN SOUP

6 chicken breasts, cooked and cubed
4 potatoes, cooked and cubed
1 cup celery, chopped
1 cup carrots, peeled and chopped
1 cup onions, chopped

3 cans cream of chicken soup
1 cup milk
1 16-oz. pkg. sliced American cheese

Place vegetables in large soup pot. Cover vegetables with water. Cook until tender. Do not pour off water. Combine cream of chicken soup and milk. Add to vegetables. Add cheese slices and stir until melted. Add cooked chicken. Season with salt and pepper. Serve warm.

Denan Cox

SPICY POTATO SOUP

1 pkg. Bear Creek Potato Soup Mix
1 pound Italian hot sausage
1 green bell pepper, diced

1 16-oz. can corn, drained
Dash of red pepper

Prepare soup according to package directions. Add diced green pepper and corn to water while soup is cooking. Meanwhile, brown sausage and drain fat. Add cooked sausage to soup. Stir in dash of red pepper.

Laura Gilgen

227

CHEESE SOUP

1 cup chicken, cooked and chopped	2 cups water
3 cups potatoes, peeled and diced	3/4 cup butter
1 cup carrots, peeled and sliced	3/4 cup flour
1 cup celery, diced	2 cups half-and-half
1/2 cup onion, chopped	2 cups milk
4 chicken bouillon cubes	1 15-oz. bottle Cheese Whiz

Combine vegetables in a large soup pot. Dissolve bouillon in water and pour over vegetables. Cook for 15-20 minutes or until vegetables are tender. In a separate pan, melt butter. Add flour and stir until smooth. Slowly add half-and-half and milk. Cook and stir over medium heat until thickened and bubbly. Stir in Cheese Whiz until melted. Stir cheese sauce into vegetables. Add cooked, chopped chicken and heat through. Serve warm.

Sharmae Gilgen

HAM AND CHEESE SOUP

Follow recipe for Cheese Soup, but substitute 1 cup cooked, chopped ham for the chicken.

Sharmae Gilgen

228

EASY CHILI

4 pounds hamburger, browned and drained

2 10-oz. cans diced tomatoes and green chilies

4 8-oz. cans tomato sauce

4 16-oz. cans chili beans

2 16-oz. cans black beans

2 envelopes chili seasoning

Combine all ingredients in a crock pot and cook on high for 1 hour.

Laura Gilgen

SOUP BREAD BOWLS

2 Tbsp. Fleishmann's fast-acting yeast

1/2 cup warm water

1 Tbsp. sugar

3 cups hot water

1/2 cup butter, softened

1/2 cup sugar

9 cups flour

2 eggs

1/2 cup powdered milk

1 Tbsp. salt

Dissolve yeast and 1 Tbsp. sugar in water. Set aside. Mix hot water, butter, and 1/2 cup sugar together. Add 3 cups flour, yeast mixture, and eggs. Mix until smooth. Stir in powdered milk, salt, and enough flour to make a moderately stiff dough. Knead for 8-10 minutes. Place in greased bowl. Let rise until double. Punch down. Let rise again. Punch down and shape into 4-inch rolls. Place on greased baking sheet at least 3 inches apart. Let rise until double. Bake at 350 for 20 minutes.

DeeAnne Gilgen

SWISS BRAID

1/4 cup scalding water
1 1/2 tsp. salt
2 tsp. yeast
1/2 cup sugar

1 1/4 cups milk
1/2 cup butter
5 3/4 cups flour
3 eggs, well beaten

Stir yeast and a pinch of sugar with scalding water in a large mixing bowl. Set aside. Heat milk and butter together until warm. Add salt and sugar and stir until dissolved. Add the beaten eggs, reserving 1 1/2 tablespoons to glaze bread. Add to yeast mixture. Stir in flour. Knead on lightly floured surface until smooth and elastic. Cover dough and let rise one hour. Punch down and lightly knead. Divide dough in half and in half again. Roll each piece into long strands, 18-20 inches long. Braid the 4 strands together. Pinch and fold under at both ends. Place on a well-greased cookie sheet. Cover and let rise until double in size (about 30-40 minutes). Gently glaze with remaining egg. Bake at 325 for 40-45 minutes or until golden brown.

This is a family bread recipe that was handed down from Great-Grandma Lena Kellenburger to Grandma Martha K. Schurter to me. We love it, and I especially love to make it if someone isn't feeling well. It may sound funny, but that is when I usually make this bread. It just makes us feel better!

Sabrina Harman Wilson

230

For a lighter meal, try sandwiches and salads. You could provide the sandwiches and ask your guests to bring a salad, hors d' oeuvres, or chips and dip.

PASTEL HAM SANDWICHES

1 loaf each of yellow, pink,
   and green bread
2 pounds ham, chopped

1 1/2 cups mayonnaise
1/4 cup mustard
6 Tbsp. sweet relish

Order sliced colored bread from a bakery. Cut crust off bread slices. Grind chopped ham in blender until finely ground. Combine with remaining ingredients. Spread ham mixture 1/4 inch thick on one side of green and yellow bread slices. Place yellow slices on green slices. Place pink slices on top. Cut sandwiches into thirds.

PASTEL EGG SANDWICHES

Follow recipe for Pastel Ham Sandwiches, but substitute 12 chopped hard-boiled eggs for the ham. To hard-boil eggs, place eggs in a large pan. Cover with luke-warm water and sprinkle with salt. Bring to a boil over medium-high heat. Turn heat off, but leave pan on stove for 5 additional minutes. Run eggs under cold water until cool enough to handle. Remove shells from eggs. Rinse eggs and chop.

CHICKEN CRESCENT ROLLS

1 1/2 cups chicken, cooked and chopped
2 8-oz. pkgs. cream cheese
2 Tbsp. ranch dressing mix (powder)
4 8-count tubes crescent rolls

Bread crumbs
1 Tbsp. Parmesan cheese
1/2 tsp. garlic salt
2 Tbsp. butter, melted

Soften cream cheese in microwave. Combine chicken, cream cheese, and ranch dressing mix together. Roll out crescent rolls. Spread large spoonful of chicken mixture in center of each roll. Roll up crescent roll and pinch edge to seal. Mix together bread crumbs, Parmesan cheese, and garlic salt. Brush rolls with melted butter and roll in bread crumb mixture. Place rolls on ungreased baking sheets. Bake at 350 for 20-25 minutes or until rolls are golden.

Lori Gilgen

CREAMY CHICKEN ROLLS

Follow first two steps as above, except omit the ranch in the cream cheese and chicken mixture. Roll out rolls and spread chicken mixture in each. Roll up and pinch edge. Bake according to crescent roll package instructions. Meanwhile, make gravy by mixing 1 can cream of chicken soup and 1/2 can milk in a saucepan. If needed, add more milk. Cook over low temperature until hot and bubbly, stirring occasionally. Pour gravy into serving container. Serve rolls with gravy and shredded cheddar cheese as toppings.

Holli Nixon

232

CHICKEN CROISSANTS

6 cups chicken, cooked and chopped

2 8-oz. pkgs. cream cheese

1 1/2 cups mayonnaise

1/2 cup Miracle Whip

6 green onions, chopped

3 celery ribs, finely diced

3 cups red grapes, halved

36 croissants, sliced

Soften cream cheese and beat until smooth. Combine with mayonnaise, Miracle Whip, green onions, celery, and grapes. Fold in chopped, cooked chicken. Spread heaping 1/4 cup of chicken salad in each croissant.

The chicken salad in this recipe can also be used to fill dollar rolls or cream puff shells (see Desserts section).

HAM AND CHEESE ROLLS

6 dozen dollar rolls, sliced in half

18 slices sandwich ham

18 slices cheddar cheese

2 cups Miracle Whip

1/3 cup yellow mustard

Cut ham and cheese slices into quarters. Mix Miracle Whip and mustard together. Spread sauce over both halves of rolls. Place one slice ham and one slice cheese on each roll bottom. Replace tops. Arrange on a serving tray.

CHICKEN, FRUIT, AND SPINACH SALAD

2 heads romaine lettuce, cut up

3-4 cups fresh spinach

1 bag Spring Mix salad

2-3 pounds chicken, cooked and marinated in Teriyaki sauce

2 cups mozzarella cheese, grated

Dressing:

1 cup canola or olive oil

1 cup apple cider vinegar

1 cup sugar

1 cup Craisins

1/2 cup strawberries, sliced

1/2 cup red grapes, halved

1 cup red onion, sliced

1 cup almonds, slivered and candied (roasted with sugar)

1/2 tsp. dry mustard

1/4 cup red onion, finely diced

1 Tbsp. poppy seeds

Toss lettuces together. Chop the marinated, cooked chicken. Toss chicken and remaining ingredients with lettuce. Blend dressing ingredients, pour over salad, and toss.

This makes a huge salad for a family gathering or pot luck.

Denan Cox

The love of a family is life's greatest blessing.

234

ZESTY PASTA SALAD

1 12-oz. bag pasta
1 4-oz. pkg. pepperoni slices
1 8-oz. pkg. American cheese
1 8-oz. pkg. mozzarella cheese
1/2 cup Parmesan cheese, grated
1 cup cherry tomatoes
1 cucumber, chopped
2 cups broccoli, chopped
1 can black olives
1 bottle Italian dressing

Cook pasta according to package directions. Cut pepperoni, American cheese, and mozzarella cheese into 1/2-inch strips. Combine all ingredients, using only enough dressing to make salad moist.

DeeAnne Gilgen

SHRIMP SALAD

1 12-oz. pkg. salad-roni
1 cup mayonnaise
2 Tbsp. ketchup
1 Tbsp. yellow mustard
2 Tbsp. Worcestershire sauce
1 rib celery, finely diced
2 sweet pickles, finely diced
1 dill pickle, finely diced
2 6-oz. cans whole baby shrimp
White pepper to taste

Cook pasta according to package directions. Drain. Rinse in cold water until pasta is cold. Drain and rinse shrimp. Combine ingredients in a large salad bowl. Serve immediately. *If I make this for a party, I mix it at the party.*

Julie Cline

GRILLED CHICKEN SALAD

3 chicken breasts, cut into strips

1 12-oz. pkg. bow-tie pasta

1 12-oz. pkg. colored spiral pasta

1 20-oz. can pineapple tidbits, drained

1 16-oz. bottle Kraft coleslaw dressing

2 cups red grapes, halved

1 cup celery, chopped

4 green onions, chopped

1 cup cashews

1 6-oz. bag Craisins

Grill chicken until done. Cut into bite-sized pieces. Cook pastas according to package directions. Drain. Combine all ingredients in a large salad bowl. Allow to sit at least 1 hour before serving.

Kimm Harman

CAESAR SALAD

2-3 heads romaine lettuce, chopped

1/2 cup Parmesan cheese, grated

2 cups cheese and garlic croutons

Lighthouse Caesar Dressing

(sold in produce section)

Chop, rinse, and pat lettuce dry. Toss with Parmesan cheese and croutons. Stir in enough dressing to lightly coat. Serve immediately. *When I bring this to a party, I bring the ingredients and mix it just before serving.*

Sharmae Gilgen

236

SARA SALAD

1 head romaine lettuce
1 head green leaf lettuce
1 head iceberg lettuce
9 Tbsp. mayonnaise
3 Tbsp. sugar

1 cup sweet peas
1/2 pound Swiss cheese, cubed
1 medium red onion, thinly sliced
1 pound bacon, cooked and crumbled

Rinse, dry, and chop lettuce. Toss lettuces together. Separate ingredients, except bacon, into three equal portions. Layer 1/3 lettuce mixture in a large salad bowl. Spread 3 Tbsp. mayonnaise on lettuce. Sprinkle with 1 Tbsp. sugar. Spread 1/3 peas, cheese, and onions on top. Starting with lettuce, repeat layers twice. Cover and refrigerate 1-6 hours. Sprinkle with crumbled bacon. Toss salad and serve.

Diane Kunz

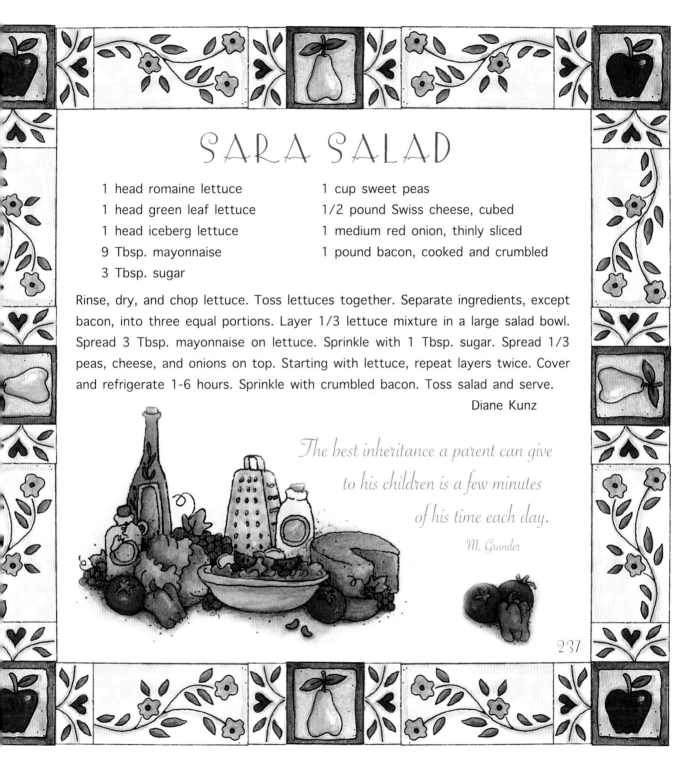

The best inheritance a parent can give to his children is a few minutes of his time each day.

M. Grander

237

DEEANNE'S FAMOUS POTATO SALAD

20 potatoes, peeled and quartered
12-13 eggs, hard-boiled
3-4 green onions, thinly sliced
4 whole dill pickles, finely diced
4-5 radishes, finely diced
3-4 stalks celery, finely diced
1 1/2 cups mayonnaise
1/2 cup ranch dressing

1/4 tsp. mace
1/4 tsp. curry powder
1/4 tsp. turmeric
1/4 tsp. cumin
1/4 tsp. dry mustard
1/4 tsp. onion powder
1/4 tsp. garlic powder
Salt and pepper

Steam potatoes until just fork-tender. Place potatoes in refrigerator until well chilled. Meanwhile, chop eggs, reserving 4-5 for the top of the salad. In a large bowl, mix remaining ingredients. Chop potatoes. Add chopped potatoes and eggs to mix and stir well. Slice remaining eggs and spread over salad. Sprinkle with turmeric and paprika.

DeeAnne's Famous Macaroni Salad

Follow above recipe, but replace potatoes with 6-8 cups cooked macaroni. Add 2 cups cooked and cubed chicken, turkey, or ham.

DeeAnne Gilgen

CREAMY CRAB DIP

1 8-oz. pkg. cream cheese
1 8-oz. pkg. imitation crab
1/2 cup mayonnaise

1 Tbsp. lemon juice
1 cup celery, chopped
2 green onions, chopped

Combine all ingredients until well blended. Serve with crackers.

Lori Gilgen

7~LAYER TACO DIP

1 can refried beans
3 ripe avocados
1 tsp. lemon juice
1/4 tsp. salt
1 cup sour cream
1 Tbsp. taco seasoning

1 cup salsa
2 cups cheese, grated
2 tomatoes, diced
1/4 cup onion, diced
1 cup olives, sliced

Spread beans in a 9x13 dish. Peel and mash three avocados. Mix lemon juice and salt with mashed avocados; spread over beans. Mix sour cream and taco seasoning together. Spread over avocados. Spread salsa over sour cream. Sprinkle grated cheese over salsa. Sprinkle diced tomatoes and onions over cheese, and place sliced olives on top. Serve with tortilla chips.

Haley Gilgen

SMOKED SALMON SNACKS

1 8-oz. pkg. cream cheese

8 ounces smoked salmon

1 16-oz. pkg. Ritz crackers

Spread a generous amount of cream cheese on each cracker and arrange on serving platter. Place small chunks of smoked salmon on top of cream cheese. Serve immediately.

Sabrina Wilson

HAM AND ONION ROLL~UPS

Spread softened cream cheese on ham slices. Place a green onion at one end. Roll up jelly-roll-style. Cut into 1-inch pieces.

BACON CHESTNUTS

2 cans whole water chestnuts

1 12-oz. bottle ketchup

1 pound bacon

Cut bacon slices in half. Wrap a bacon slice around each water chestnut. Secure with toothpick. Arrange in 9x13 baking dish. Pour entire bottle of ketchup over top. Bake at 350 for 1 hour.

Stan Stokes

240

ARTICHOKE DIP

1 can artichoke hearts
1 jar marinated artichoke hearts
1 4-oz. can chopped green chilies

1/2 cup mayonnaise
3-4 dashes hot pepper sauce
1 cup cheddar cheese, shredded

Chop artichoke hearts. Combine all ingredients except 1/2 cup cheese. Spread mixture in small pan and sprinkle with remaining cheese. Bake at 375 for 12-15 minutes. Serve with tortilla chips.

Kodi Gilgen

YOGURT FRUIT DIP

2 8-oz. cups Yoplait peach yogurt
1 16-oz. container Cool Whip

Combine yogurt and Cool Whip together.
Serve with fresh fruit, such as
apples, bananas, cantaloupe, grapes,
honeydew, kiwifruit, peaches,
pineapple, strawberries, or
watermelon.

Laura Gilgen

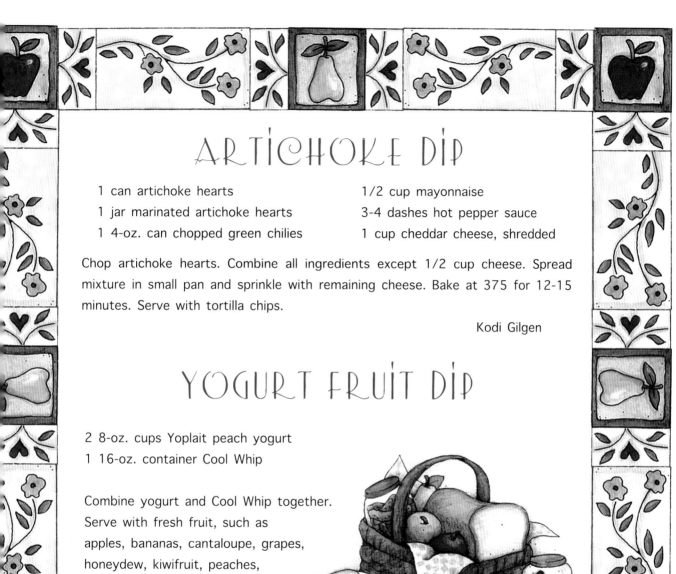

241

FROG~EYE SALAD

2 30-oz. cans fruit cocktail
6 cans mandarin oranges
1/2 box Acini de pepe pasta
1 6-oz. pkg. Jell-O (any flavor)

1 16-oz. container Cool Whip
1 24-oz. container cottage cheese
1/2 bag miniature marshmallows

Drain fruit cocktail and mandarin oranges; shake strainer to get liquid completely out of fruit. Cook Acini de pepe pasta according to package directions. Drain pasta and cool. Blend Jell-O (reserve some for sprinkling) and fruit. Mix with Cool Whip. Stir in cottage cheese and marshmallows. Fold in cooled pasta until well blended. Sprinkle with reserved Jell-O. Use immediately or refrigerate until ready to serve.

DeeAnne Gilgen

GRANDPA'S JELL~O

1 6-oz. box Jell-O (any flavor)
1 cup water

1 16- 20-oz. can fruit (any kind)
1 8-oz. pkg. cream cheese

Boil water in saucepan. Stir in Jell-O until dissolved. Blend fruit and cream cheese in blender until smooth. Add Jell-O and blend until well mixed. Pour into serving dish and refrigerate 3-4 hours or until firm. You may substitute 2 cups fresh fruit for canned; increase water to 1 1/2 cups.

Denny Harman

RASPBERRY SHERBET

2 half-gallon cartons pineapple sherbet, softened
1 16-oz. bag or 2 8-oz. boxes frozen raspberries

5 bananas, peeled
and sliced

Mix all ingredients. Freeze until ready to serve.

Lori Gilgen

BLUEBERRY SMOOTHIES

4 Tbsp. blueberry-pomegranate juice
1 cup milk

3 scoops vanilla ice cream

Put all ingredients in blender. Blend until smooth.
You can use any fruit juice in this recipe, but blueberry-pomegranate is my favorite.

Jefferson Beals

COLORED ICE CUBES

2 pkgs. Kool-Aid, any flavor
2 cups sugar

2 3-liter bottles Sprite

Make Kool-Aid according to package directions. Pour into ice cube trays. Freeze.
Mix with Sprite in a punch bowl or glass pitcher.
I usually make these at our Christmas Eve party using red and green Kool-Aid.

Kimm Harman

FLAG~TWIRLER CHEESECAKE

2 8-oz pkgs. cream cheese, softened
1 1/2 cups powdered sugar
2 envelopes Dream Whip whipped topping
2 cups milk
2 graham cracker crusts
1 21-oz. can pie filling

Mix cream cheese and powdered sugar with a hand mixer until smooth. In a separate bowl, mix Dream Whip according to package directions. Combine with cream cheese mixture. Pour into crust. Freeze for 2-3 hours or until firm. Before serving, spread pie filling on top.

MILLION~DOLLAR FUDGE

1 can evaporated milk
2 cups sugar
1/2 cup butter
3 12-oz. pkgs. chocolate chips
1 pint marshmallow cream
1 tsp. vanilla
Nuts (opt.)

Combine milk, sugar, and butter in medium saucepan. Cook and stir over medium heat until mixture boils. Remove from heat. Stir in vanilla and pour over remaining ingredients. Stir well. If desired, stir in nuts.

Louise Beals

OATMEAL FUDGE BARS

1 cup shortening	1 tsp. baking powder
2 cups brown sugar	1 tsp. salt
2 eggs, well beaten	1 1/2 cups flour
1 tsp. vanilla	4 cups oatmeal
Filling:	
1 12-oz. package chocolate chips	1 tsp. vanilla
1 can sweetened condensed milk	1/4 tsp. salt
2 Tbsp. butter	

Combine ingredients until well blended. Reserve 1/2 mixture for top. Press into bottom of large cookie sheet. Mix all filling ingredients in a saucepan. Cook and stir over low heat until melted. Spread over crust. Top with reserved crumbs. Bake at 350 for 15 minutes. Cut into squares.

Denan Cox

OATMEAL BUTTERSCOTCH BARS

Follow directions for Oatmeal Fudge Bars, but substitute 1 12-oz. package butterscotch chips for the chocolate chips.

LEMON COOKIES

2 boxes lemon cake mix   1 8-oz. container Cool Whip
2 medium eggs   Powdered sugar

Blend cake mix, eggs, and Cool Whip. Roll dough into balls. Roll balls in powdered sugar and place on ungreased cookie sheet. Bake at 350 for 7-8 minutes. Do not let cookies brown.

Aubrey Beals

SOFT CHOCOLATE CHIP COOKIES

1 cup shortening   2 cups flour
1 cup brown sugar, packed   1 tsp. baking soda
1/2 cup granulated sugar   1 tsp. salt
1 tsp. vanilla   2 cups chocolate chips
2 eggs, well beaten

Cream first 4 ingredients. Add eggs and mix well. Sift dry ingredients into a separate bowl. Add to creamed mixture and stir until fluffy. Stir in chocolate chips. Drop onto ungreased cookie sheet 2 inches apart. Bake at 375 for 8 minutes. Cool on cookie sheet 2-3 minutes, then place on wire rack to cool.

Tara Gilgen

246

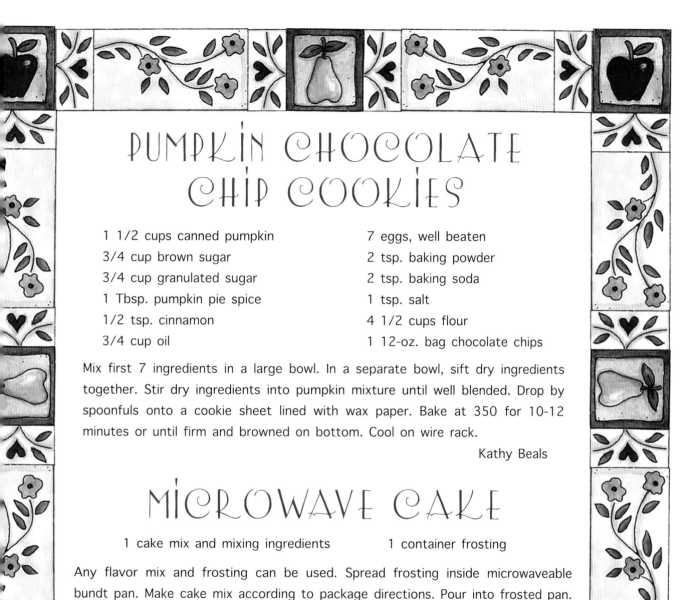

PUMPKIN CHOCOLATE CHIP COOKIES

1 1/2 cups canned pumpkin	7 eggs, well beaten
3/4 cup brown sugar	2 tsp. baking powder
3/4 cup granulated sugar	2 tsp. baking soda
1 Tbsp. pumpkin pie spice	1 tsp. salt
1/2 tsp. cinnamon	4 1/2 cups flour
3/4 cup oil	1 12-oz. bag chocolate chips

Mix first 7 ingredients in a large bowl. In a separate bowl, sift dry ingredients together. Stir dry ingredients into pumpkin mixture until well blended. Drop by spoonfuls onto a cookie sheet lined with wax paper. Bake at 350 for 10-12 minutes or until firm and browned on bottom. Cool on wire rack.

Kathy Beals

MICROWAVE CAKE

1 cake mix and mixing ingredients   1 container frosting

Any flavor mix and frosting can be used. Spread frosting inside microwaveable bundt pan. Make cake mix according to package directions. Pour into frosted pan. Microwave on high 12 minutes. Dump onto plate. Sprinkle with powdered sugar (optional).

Kimm Harman

ROCKY ROAD BROWNIES

1 cup butter
1/3 cup cocoa
2 cups sugar
4 eggs
2 tsp. vanilla

1 1/2 cups flour
1/2 cup walnuts, chopped (opt.)
1/2 pkg. miniature marshmallows
1 container chocolate frosting

Combine first 3 ingredients until well mixed. Stir in eggs, one at a time. Stir in vanilla. Stir in flour and nuts (optional). Pour into a greased 9x13 pan. Bake at 350 for 24-34 minutes (don't overcook). Spread marshmallows evenly over top. Return to oven for 30 seconds. Frost when completely cooled.

Denan Cox

BANANA CAKE

4 ripe bananas, mashed
1/2 cup shortening
1 cup sugar
1 tsp. soda

2 eggs
1 1/2 cups flour
1 tsp. vanilla

Cream shortening and sugar. Dissolve soda in 1 Tbsp. hot water. Add to bananas. Combine all ingredients. Spread in a greased and floured 9x13 cake pan. Bake at 350 for 30-35 minutes or until toothpick inserted near center comes out clean.

Martha Schurter

248

GOLDEN SWEET CHEX MIX

1 cup light corn syrup	1/2 box Rice Chex
1 cup sugar	3/4 box Golden Grahams
1 cup butter	1 cup slivered almonds
1 tsp. vanilla	2 cups flaked coconut

Combine first 3 ingredients in a saucepan. Bring to a boil. Boil for 2 minutes. Remove from heat and stir in vanilla. Combine remaining ingredients in a large bowl. Pour syrup over cereal mixture. Toss to coat.

Kimm Harman

SCOTCHEROOS

1 cup light corn syrup	6 cups Rice Krispies
1 cup sugar	1 cup butterscotch chips
1 1/2 cups peanut butter	1 cup chocolate chips

Combine first 3 ingredients in a saucepan. Bring to a boil, stirring constantly to avoid burning. Pour over cereal and mix. Press into a greased 9x13 pan. Sprinkle butterscotch and chocolate chips on top. Heat in oven or microwave just until chips are melted enough to spread evenly. Cool and cut into squares.

Ann Harman

249